Evelyn Waugh

NINETY-TWO DAYS

Penguin Books

Penguin Books Ltd, Harmondsworth, Middlesex, England
Viking Penguin Inc., 40 West 23rd Street, New York, New York 10010, U.S.A.
Penguin Books Australia Ltd, Ringwood, Victoria, Australia
Penguin Books Canada Ltd, 2801 John Street, Markham, Ontario, Canada L3R 1B4
Penguin Books (N.Z.) Ltd, 182–190 Wairau Road, Auckland 10, New Zealand

First published by Duckworth 1934
Published in Penguin Books 1985
Copyright © Evelyn Waugh 1934
All rights reserved

Made and printed in Great Britain by
Richard Clay (The Chaucer Press) Ltd,
Bungay, Suffolk
Filmset in 10/12 pt Monophoto Baskerville by
Northumberland Press Ltd, Gateshead
Tyne and Wear

CONTENTS

ONE

OCTOBER 12TH, 1933

At last, relentlessly, inevitably, the lugubrious morning has dawned; day of wrath which I have been postponing week by week for five months.

Late last evening I arrived at the house I have borrowed and established myself in absolute solitude in the deserted nurseries; this morning immediately after breakfast I arranged the writing table with a pile of foolscap, clean blotting paper, a full inkpot, folded maps, a battered journal and a heap of photographs; then in very low spirits I smoked a pipe and read two newspapers, walked to the village post office in search of Relief nibs, returned and brooded with disgust over the writing table, smoked another pipe and wrote two letters, walked into the paddock and looked at a fat pony; then back to the writing table. It was the end of the tether. There was nothing for it but to start writing this book.

I read the other day that when his biographer revealed that Trollope did his work by the clock, starting regularly as though at an office and stopping, even in the middle of a sentence, when his time was up, there was an immediate drop in his reputation and sales. People in his time believed the romantic legend of inspired genius; they enjoyed the idea of the wicked artist – Rossetti unhinged by chloral, closeted with women of low repute, or Swinburne sprawling under the table; they respected the majestic and august, Tennyson, Carlyle and Ruskin in white whiskers and black cloaks; what they could not believe was that anyone who lived like themselves, got up and went to bed methodically and turned out a regular quantity of work a day, could possibly write anything worth reading.

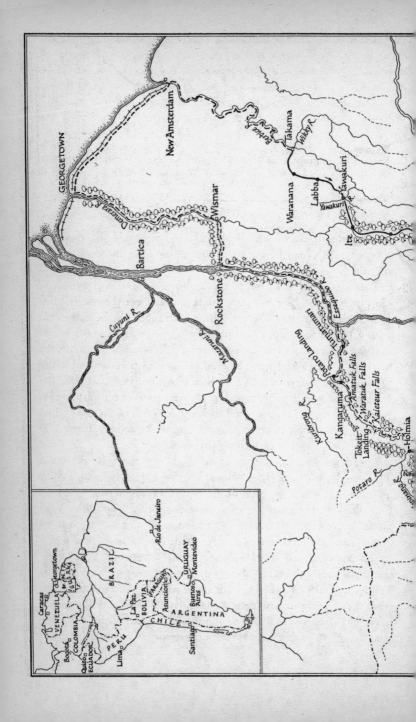

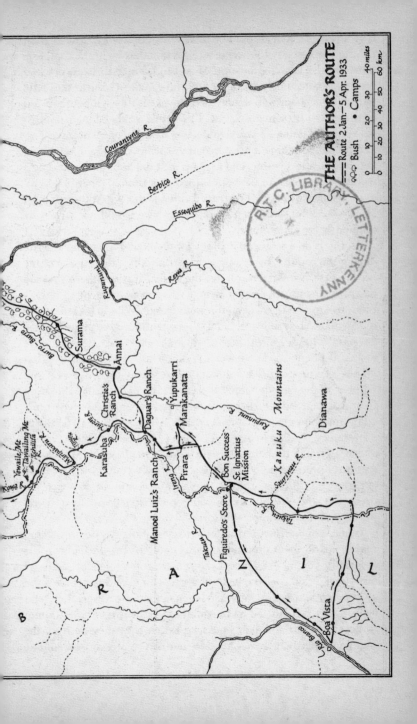

THE AUTHOR'S ROUTE

═══ Route 2 Jan.–5 Apr. 1933

⌒⌒⌒ Bush   • Camps

0 10 20 30 40 miles
0 10 20 30 40 50 60 km

Courantyne R.

Berbice R.

Essequibo R.

Rupununi R.

Rewa R.

Surama

Annai

Christie's Ranch

Daguar's Ranch

Yupukarri

Marakanata

Karasuba

Manoel Luiz's Ranch

Pirara

Bon Success

St Ignatius Mission

Figuiredo's Store

Takutu R.

Kanuku Mountains

Rupununi R.

Saurwau R.

Takutu R.

Dianawa

Yewaile Mt.

Tawaiing Mt.

Echilu

Kowa R.

Maruranaw R.

Kuiuni R.

B   R   A   Z   I   L

Boa Vista

Rio Branco

Nowadays, of course, opinion is all the other way. The highest tribute one can pay to success is to assume that an author employs someone else to write for him. Most Englishmen dislike work and grumble about their jobs and writers now make it so clear they hate writing, that their public may become excusably sympathetic and urge them to try something else. I have seldom met a male novelist who enjoyed doing his work, and never heard of one who gave it up and took to anything more congenial. I believe it would have been better for trade if writers had kept up the bluff about inspiration. As it is the tendency is to the opposite exaggeration of regarding us all as mercenary drudges. The truth I think is this – that though most of us would not write except for money, we would not write any differently for more money.

All this is, in a sense, an apology for the book I am going to write during the coming, miserable weeks. It is to be a description of the way I spent last winter and, on the face of it, since there were no hairbreadth escapes, no romances, no discoveries, it seems presumptuous to suppose that I shall interest anyone. Who in his senses will read, still less buy, a travel book of no scientific value about a place he has no intention of visiting? (I will make a present of that sentence to any ill-intentioned reviewer.) Well, the answer as I see it, is that man is a communicative animal; that probably there are a certain number of people who enjoy the same kind of things as I do, and that an experience which for me was worth six months of my time, a fair amount of money and a great deal of exertion may be worth a few hours' reading to others. Just as a carpenter, I suppose, seeing a piece of rough timber feels an inclination to plane it and square it and put it into shape, so a writer is not really content to leave any experience in the amorphous, haphazard condition in which life presents it; and putting an experience into shape means, for a writer, putting it into communicable form.

When anyone hears that a writer is going to do something that seems to them unusual, such as going to British Guiana, the invariable comment is, 'I suppose you are going to collect material for a book,' and since no one but a prig can take the trouble to be always explaining his motives, it is convenient to answer, 'Yes,' and leave it at that. But the truth is that self-respecting writers do not 'collect material' for their books, or rather that they do it all the time in living their lives. One does not travel, any more than one falls in love, to collect material. It is simply part of one's life. Some writers have a devotion for rural England; they settle in Sussex, identify themselves with the village, the farm, and the hedgerow and, inevitably, they write about it; others move into high society; for myself and many better than me, there is a fascination in distant and barbarous places, and particularly in the borderlands of conflicting cultures and states of development, where ideas, uprooted from their traditions, become oddly changed in transplantation. It is there that I find the experiences vivid enough to demand translation into literary form.

So for the next month or two I shall be reliving my journey in Guiana and Brazil. Not that it has ever been out of my memory. It has been there, ill digested, throughout a crowded and fretful summer, obtruding itself in a fragmentary way at incongruous moments. Now, in this seaside nursery, it will be all laid out, like the maps and photographs and drawings on the writing table, while falling leaves in the autumnal sunshine remind me that it will soon be time to start out again somewhere else.

DECEMBER, 1932

Warm sun, calm water, a slight following wind; after a week of heavy seas it was at last possible to write. Passengers, hitherto invisible, appeared from below and started playing deck games. There was no band. The ship was small, old and slow, a cargo boat carrying a few passengers and not caring much about them. It was not until the sea became smooth that one saw how slow she was. A more comfortable ship would have necessitated transhipping at Trinidad.

The company was, presumably, typical of the route; three or four planters returning to the islands, men of old-fashioned appearance, thin brown faces and bulky watch-chains; two parsons, one white, one black, both affable; two English soaks doing the 'round trip' for the good of their health, both surly when sober; some nondescript women of various colours rejoining husbands or visiting brothers; an agreeable English family on holiday, every day of their winter carefully planned in advance; a genteel young Negress with purple lips; a somewhat cranky young man from the Philippines who had an attachment for islands. Very few were going as far as Georgetown.

The first night of the voyage was as depressing a time as I have

11

known in adult life. We sailed from London Docks. It was intensely cold; the heating apparatus was out of order and the bar was closed until we were at sea. Most people have some reason to be sad when it actually comes to leaving. At dusk there was a boat drill; depressed, mutually suspicious passengers paraded in rows opposite ragged and shivering lascars; all round us colourless water and colourless Thames-side factories. That was the low spot of the journey; everything after it was a holiday.

For those of us who were good sailors, that is to say. From the time we got into the Channel until a day past the Azores, the boat rolled and wallowed extravagantly. There are many other disadvantages in rough weather besides seasickness: the noise is incessant; every movement becomes an exertion; it is difficult to sleep; the stewards become facetious. Rough weather performs the highly desirable function, however, of keeping the children quiet; for it is notorious that children, at sea in fine weather, are one of the traveller's most severe trials.

During the first ten days I began to read up a little more about the place I was going to. I could scarcely have known less to start with, and when people immediately before my departure asked, 'But why British Guiana?' I was at difficulties to find an answer, except that I was going *because* I knew so little; and also because it has always attracted me on the map.

When I was at school there was no question of Geography being taught badly or not enough; it simply was not taught at all and arriving as a History scholar at Oxford I earned the immediate and implacable disapproval of my tutor through revealing that I did not know which way the Rhine flowed. Since then I have picked up a little, but far less, I imagine, than a bright elementary schoolboy knows. I looked at *The Times* shipping news today and read that the *Bideford* had left Henjam and arrived at Basidu, the *Cumberland* was at Beppu, the *Dauntless* at Ushuwaia, the *Fitzroy* at Lerwick, the *Ladybird* at Kiukiang, and the *Scarborough* at New Bedford, and reflected despondently that none of these places meant a thing to me. I am shaky about solstices and equinoxes. If required to explain how tides work I should find myself in hopeless confusion. On the other hand I do greatly enjoy browsing over atlases, and for years the Guianas have fascinated me.

It always seemed odd that those three little gobs of empire should survive in the general explosion of South American self-government. Cayenne was always in the news through its association with Devil's Island; Dutch Guiana conveyed nothing, but that is scarcely surprising since no normally educated Englishman knows anything about Dutch colonies; British Guiana seemed absurdly remote. One is always meeting Canadians and Australians; everyone has cousins in Kenya and Nigeria and Rhodesia, South Africans seem to have controlled English life twenty-five years ago; people are constantly going and coming to and from the Malay States and India; one way or another most of the Empire (and particularly Tristan da Cunha) comes to one's notice at some time; but I never remember hearing anything at all about Guiana.

Then I met a sailor who told some astonishing stories about the natives of New Guinea, and, as I had listened inattentively to the first part of the conversation, that set me thinking about Guiana. By the time I discovered my mistake I had got interested in the place for other reasons. I bought a large map of it and found it all blanks and guesses; I found that a friend of mine had had an uncle there as a missionary; another had himself made a journey up one of the rivers to Kaieteur Falls, one of the finest, most inaccessible, and least advertised natural wonders of the world. I met someone else who had business interests all along the coast and spoke of a journey anywhere in the interior as a very reckless undertaking. I collected the few books that dealt with the country. And so gradually a vague, general idea began to take shape in my mind of a large empty territory stretching up three great rivers and their tributaries to shadowy, undefined boundaries; most of it was undeveloped and unsurveyed, large areas quite unexplored; except for a trace of grass land on the Brazilian frontier, and an inhabited fringe along the coast, it was all forest or swamp; there was no railway or road into the interior, the only means of communication being by boat up rivers broken every few miles by rapids and falls; the coast population contained every conceivable race, chiefly Portuguese, Negro and East Indian; the greater part of the colony had no permanent inhabitants, except shy little communities of aboriginal Indians; except on the coast there had been practically no European settlement and little enough there; and a few place names, later to become real, stuck in my mind as words – Bartika, Wismar, Rupununi, Takutu.

There had been a constitution but finding it unworkable they reverted to Crown Colony Government. The coastal strip was much like any West Indian island slightly down at heel; the interior, virgin forest of the sort that stretches over half the continent. So much I had gathered from conversation and cursory reading. It was new country to me and after alternating panics that it would prove impossibly arduous or impossibly dull, I abandoned the other winter projects that had been floating vaguely in my mind – the Solomon Islands, fox-hunting, carpentry classes, Iraq and Mexico – and took my ticket to Georgetown, with two small suitcases, a camera, a letter of credit and no clear plan of what my procedure would be when I arrived.

My fellow passengers from Georgetown were not encouraging. They were mildly excited at first when they learned that anyone who wrote books was coming to their country, and with that pathetic belief in the might of the pen which one continually meets in out-of-the-way places, hoped that I should persuade the Imperial Government to 'do something' about local trade conditions. The country was stiff with gold and diamonds, they said, which only needed 'development'. When I told them that I wanted to go up-country, they lost interest. Of course there was always Kaieteur, they said, quite a lot of tourists went there; three or four a year; they believed it was very pretty when you got there but it cost a great deal and you might be drowned or get fever; or there was the Rupununi savannah; several white people lived there and even a white woman, but it cost a great deal to get there and you might be drowned on the way or get fever; besides it was only at certain seasons you could get there at all. I had far better winter in Trinidad, they said, where there was an excellent new country club, horse races and a lot of money about or at Barbados where the bathing was unrivalled.

And to be honest I did gaze rather wistfully as each of the islands in turn disappeared behind us. The first was Antigua and, coming on it as we did after twelve days of unbroken horizons, it remains the most vivid and most glamorous. Not that there was anything particularly remarkable about it – steep little hills covered in bush, a fringe of palm along the beach, brilliant blue water revealing, fathoms down, the silver sand of its bed; an old fort covering the bay; a shabby little town of wooden, balconied houses, its only prominent building a large plain cathedral rebuilt after an earth-quake, with shining towers and a good pitch-pine interior; inquisitive black urchins in the street; women in absurd sun hats, the brims drooping and flapping over their black faces, waddling along on flat feet; ragged Negroes lounging aimlessly at corners; baskets of highly coloured fish for sale – purple and scarlet like markings of a mandril; ramshackle motor cars; and in the churchyard the memorials of a lost culture – the rococo marble tombs of forgotten sugar planters, carved in England and imported by sailing ship in the golden days of West Indian prosperity.

It is significant that marble, that most grand and delicate of all building material, the substance of almost all sculpture, has today become the symbol of the vulgar and garish – the profiteers of *Punch circa* 1920, Lyons Corner House and the Victor Emmanuel Memorial; it is part of the flight from magnificence to which both the 'ye-olde'-pewter-and-sampler aesthetic and its more recent counterpart, the 'modern'-concrete-and-steel-tube, have given im-petus. A broken column in the Syrian desert, an incised slab overwhelmed in the gross vegetation of the South American bush remain as spoors of something gracious that passed that way centu-ries before. I thought how delightful it would be to make a study of the trade in marble and rare stones, tracing the course round the Mediterranean cities of the porphyry galleys from the hottest quarries in the world on the Red Sea coast; a trade so active that practically no porphyry has been quarried since and all the pedestals and urns of Napoleonic bric-à-brac were made, so I am told, of stone cut in the time of Caligula. But this is the kind of thing one thinks about only when one is travelling; all the time that I am abroad I make resolutions to study one thing or another when I get back – Portuguese, map-making, photography; nothing ever comes of it. Perhaps it is a good thing to preserve one's ignorance for old age.

We stopped only a day at Antigua to put down passengers and cargo; one of the things we brought to the islands was holly for their Christmas decorations. It looked odd being tossed down into the lighters under a blazing sky, so completely dissociated from its traditional concomitants of Yule logs and whisky punch and Santa Claus stamping off the snow. But it was not my first Christmas in the tropics; I knew it all – the cablegram forms specially decorated with berries and robins, the puzzled native children before the crib

15

in the church, 'Auld Lang Syne' on the gramophone, the beggars trotting hopefully behind one in the street saying 'Happy Clistmas – me velly Clistian boy'; the prospect of hot plum pudding on a windless, steaming evening. But everyone all the world over has something to be melancholy about at Christmas, not on account of there being anything intrinsically depressing about the feast but because it is an anniversary too easily memorable; one can cast back one's mind and remember where one was, and in what company, every year from the present to one's childhood.

For the last week of the voyage the life of the ship disintegrated. Most of the day we were on land; the decks were crowded with agents; passengers disappeared and new ones arrived on short journeys between the islands; even the soaks in the bar once got as far as the nearest hotel ashore. I should like to write about the islands, particularly Barbados with its castellated churches, 'poor white' descendants of Monmouth's army, its excellent ghost story and overrated cooking – but there is a reason why I should not. My brother Alec is also fond of travelling and like me, poor fish, he lives by writing books, so on one of our rare but agreeable meetings we made a compact each to keep off the other's territory; with a papal gesture he made me a present of the whole of Africa and a good slice of Asia in exchange for the Polynesian Islands, North America and the West Indies. When he saw in a newspaper that I was going to Guiana he sent me a sharp note claiming that the West Indies included any places on the mainland of West Indian character i.e., sugar estates, slaves, rum and pirates – and recommending British Honduras. We compromised on my promising to get up-country as soon as I could and to pay as little attention as possible to what I passed on the way. It is an odd thing about my brother and me that though we scarcely ever meet each other in England and seem to share none of the same friends, I often come upon his tracks abroad. This occurred in Trinidad in quite a startling way.

I was sitting, an hour or so after our arrival, on the verandah of the principal hotel, talking to some acquaintances I had picked up.

It seemed to me a good hotel; there was plenty of coming and going and a constant fanfare of motor horns, two men competed to take your hat and did not give you a number, a blackboard announced the local sailings, there was a stall selling American illustrated magazines at a greatly enhanced price, drinks were extremely expensive, there were numerous servants doing nothing and half the tables were occupied by lonely and fretful men waiting for people who had not turned up; it had in fact all the character-istics – whether you like them or not is a different matter – that the rough and tumble of life has taught one to associate with a good hotel.

We had a round or two of swizzles and then one of my new friends said, 'I say, your name is mud in this joint.'

'It stinks,' said the other.

Now one may or may not be used to this sort of thing by the end of one's stay in a place, but this seemed too early days for anyone to have taken against me; it sounded like mere prejudice; so I asked the reason.

'Well, that book you wrote,' he said, 'laying into this hotel. I don't say you were wrong, but you can hardly expect them to like it here.'

Then I remembered that in one of his books my brother had dealt at some length with the discomforts he had suffered in an hotel in Trinidad. Apparently this busy place where we were sitting was the original of his 'Baracuta'. There had been a legal action about it, not against him but against a member of the local parliament who had quoted him. And while this was being explained to me, a message arrived that the manager had heard I was in the hotel and was coming to talk to me. A difficult moment.

'He's quite a decent chap,' my companions explained, 'except when he gets roused.'

'Here he comes.'

A stocky, neat man, not, as it happened, unlike my brother, was approaching in a purposeful way. 'Good evening, Mr Waugh,' he said. 'I heard you were here. Boy, take an order for drinks' and then turning with what I took to be an ugly glint in his eye he said, 'I hope you like my hotel better than your brother did.'

We had a drink and talked uncomfortably about my destination in Guiana. There was clearly going to be no chucking out, but there was still the glint in the manager's eye.

Presently I said, 'I hope Alec's book didn't cause you much trouble.'

'Trouble? I got two hundred and fifty quid damages for it. I could do with some more trouble like that. Boy, take an order for drinks.' Then I realized that the glint was far from menacing. We had some

17

more drinks and he made me a member of his country club. Finally he said, 'Look here, I feel I owe your family something for the good turn your brother did me. Why go back to the ship? They'll be taking on cargo all night and it'll be as noisy as hell. Stay here as my guest.'

I murmured that I had brought no luggage ashore.

'That's all right. I'll fix you up.'

So that night after a heavy evening at the country club – which was all stiff shirts and white waistcoats and saxophones and as urban as the Embassy – I went back to a large suite at the 'Baracuta' and found put out for me silk pyjamas, a dressing gown gayer than I should have dared choose for myself, a new toothbrush, and a note begging me to call for anything else I needed. An exemplary manner in which to accept criticism.

Blue water ends at Trinidad; there and from there onwards the sea is murky; opaque, dingy stuff the colour of shabby stucco, thick with mud sweeping down from the great continental rivers – the Orinoco, the Essequibo, the Demerara, the Berbice, the Courantyne; all along the coast their huge mouths gape amidst dune and mangrove, pouring out into the blue Caribbean the waters of the remote highlands. Later I was to tramp across part of the great continental divide, where the tributaries of the Amazon and Essequibo dovetail into one another, tiny cascading brooks, confusing in an unmapped country because they seemed always to be flowing in the direction one did not expect; I was to wade through them or scramble over them on slippery tree-trunks in the forest where they were ruby clear, wine-coloured from the crimson timber; I was to paddle tedious days down them when they had become deep and black; leaving them months later, as I saw the water become blue and clear again I was to feel touched with regret, for they had become for a time part of my life. But now as we approached the mainland I only felt mildly depressed that bathing had ceased to be attractive.

Depression deepened as rain set in; a monotonous tropical downpour, always dreary, most monotonous and most depressing when one is on the water. We were already a day late and now we missed the tide by an hour and had to lie at anchor in the rain and a slight fog, waiting to cross the bar into Demerara. There was a lightship faintly visible a mile or so away. They told me without pride that it was a new one. There were now only a handful of passengers left, all pretty impatient at the delay.

Next day, before noon, we arrived. There was nothing to see. The town lies at the mouth of the Demerara on the right bank; opposite are low, green mangrove swamps. Half a dozen small ships lay alongside the quay. We steamed up and then drifted down to our berth with the current. Low wooden sheds and low roofs beyond them; everything quite flat; rain streamed down ceaselessly. I have never seen a less attractive harbour; hope dried up in one at the sight of it; only the heavy reek of sugar occupied the senses.

Landing was simple. There was none of the jaunty cross-examination which usually greets a British subject when he arrives on British territory; an elderly Negro in a straw hat glanced at our passports; the Customs officers opened nothing; we passed through the sheds, which were full of bees attracted to the sugar bags, and out into the water-logged street; a taxi splashed and skidded to the hotel; the windows were obscured by rain.

A bare bedroom with white wooden walls, a large bed with mosquito netting, a rocking chair, a faint smell of 'Flit'. There I was.

People sometimes ask me, no doubt by way of politeness and to make conversation, 'But when you arrive alone at these out-of-the-way places, what do you *do?* I mean how do you *start?*' Well, apart from its conversational value in keeping one going another ten minutes, that is a good question and I have often wondered if there is a satisfactory answer. On this particular occasion the first thing I did was to change my hotel. Not that there was anything wrong with the one that had been chosen for me, in the sense that Alec found things wrong with his 'Baracuta'. Residents considered it the best in the town. The man with business interests mentioned before had booked me a room there; it was clean and quiet and select and full in the sea breeze, but it simply would not do. I have picked up enough about travelling to know that when one arrives in a strange town the thing one needs is a very noisy and busy hotel, with people from out of town popping into the bar for drinks and elderly men telling stories until late into the night. There was one like that in Georgetown and I got into it that afternoon. It was kept by a dashing, handsome fellow with a military title, half Irish and half Portuguese, with a fine swagger and plenty of talk. There I removed my luggage to a bare bedroom with white wooden walls, a large bed with mosquito netting, a rocking chair and a faint smell of 'Flit', and felt comforted by the change.

Two coloured reporters arrived from local newspapers to interview me. They had followed me on bicycles from the other hotel. (This, let me hasten to say, is no indication of fame. All first-class passengers are given column interviews on arrival at Georgetown.) They looked rather damp and had none of the breezy technique of their trade. They took down all I said laboriously as though I were a witness at an archbishop's court.

Was it true that I was a writer? Yes.

A writer who had published books or just a writer? I told them that I did write books but that I had also been a reporter for three weeks on the *Daily Express*. The London *Express*? That clearly impressed them, confirming what I have always maintained, that most fools can get a book published but it takes a particular kind of fool to hold down a job on a daily paper.

Was I going to write about Guiana? One of them had a cutting from a London paper in which I had facetiously said that I understood the beetles in Guiana were as big as pigeons and that one killed them with shot-guns. Had I really come to shoot beetles, they asked? They were afraid I should be disappointed. The beetles were certainly remarkably large, but not as large as that.

Had I any views about the mineral resources of the country? When I confessed that I had not, they were clearly nonplussed; this was their stock, foolproof question, because most visitors to Georgetown came there with some idea of prospecting for diamonds or gold. They gazed at me with reproach. I volunteered the information that I was going up-country.

'Ah, to Kaieteur?'

I then inwardly took the vow which I very nearly kept, that I would in no circumstances visit that very famous waterfall. I told them that my route was so far uncertain but that I hoped to travel up into Brazil and out by the Amazon. They took it all down but they looked incredulous. Then they shut up their notebooks and wished me a happy journey. They knew better than me. I was going to Kaieteur all right.

So I was left to tackle the old problem of getting through the afternoon, which, next to the problem of getting through the morning, is one of the hardest a lonely man can set himself.

There was nothing particular to do; there never is on occasions of this kind, so I did what one always does. I wrote my name in the book at Government House, presented my only letter of introduction (the recipient was away; they always are), set off some affectionate cablegrams (decorated with holly and robins this time and at a reduced rate, in honour of Christmas) and, since the rain had stopped, set out on foot to see the town.

Perhaps it was the name Georgetown, so like that of an Irish country house, that made me expect something different. Anyway for no better reason that I can think of, I had pictured the place small and solid like the town at St Helena. Instead it was all made of wood and very large; large in the tiresome sense that everything was a long way from everything else. The main streets were very broad, with grass and trees down the centre, and the houses all 'stood in their own grounds'. The shops were large departmental stores and seemed all to be called either Booker's or Foggarty's; the club, for which I had found a temporary membership card awaiting me, was a vast barn entirely empty. The museum took some finding; it was an upper floor smelling of must and containing a few cases of Indian work, some faded photographs and the worst stuffed animals I have seen anywhere. There was a large Catholic cathedral, concrete and unfinished, and numerous timber churches in the box-of-bricks style of architecture. The people seemed all black or brown; the black noisy and shabby, the brown subdued and natty. There had once been trams but they had ceased working. That at first sight was Georgetown.†

Subsequent closer acquaintance could not improve the architecture but it revealed a number of very likeable qualities in the life of the place. Acknowledgements of kindness received tend to make rather tedious reading but it would be churlish to omit any reference to the cordiality and help which I encountered from every kind of person in British Guiana; much of this will, I hope, be apparent in the ensuing narrative; one thing I would like to remark on particularly. It is delightful but not uncommon to receive some

---

† Doubtless some local patriot will complain that I give a wrong impression; that there is a cricket club, a promenade along the sea front and a spacious botanical gardens. That is all true. I have nothing against the amenities of the place. Just the reverse, that it is disappointing to travel a long way and find at the end of one's journey, a well-laid-out garden city.

hospitality from British officials abroad; it is because His Excellency the Governor and Lady Denham extended to me so much more than the formal courtesies of their position, that I should like to offer them here my explicit and especial thanks.

It was December 22nd when I landed, and January 3rd when I left for the interior. Most of this time, with the exception of three delightful days spent in the Governor's launch on an expedition up the Essequibo mouth to Mazaruni station, was spent in trying to make some sort of plans for the future. Christmas was both a good and a bad time for this purpose; good because most of the people from up country had come down to town for the celebrations, bad because they took the holidays seriously in Georgetown and most of the shops and offices were shut most of the time. Most of my information came casually from conversation in the hotel bar; indeed so much of one's help comes in that way that I wonder how teetotallers ever get about at all.

Gradually I picked up some of the vocabulary of the place and since I shall be using it in future, it will be as well to give some explanation. First as to the races. In East Africa people are divided into Europeans, Indians and natives. In Guiana the word 'native' is never used. The aboriginal Indians are called Indians or 'bucks'. The Indians, that is to say the descendants of the indentured immigrants from India, are called East Indians; there are great numbers of these, mostly in agricultural village communities along the coast; then there are the Negro and mulatto descendants of emancipated slaves who are usually spoken of as blacks and coloured people. I never heard 'nigger' used except familiarly by one black to another. Creole is used of anybody, black, coloured or white, born in the West Indies, and also of animals bred there. Then there are the whites, who in Guiana are practically all temporary inhabitants, officials and business men on a job; there is no white Creole aristocracy such as one finds in the islands. The English are, I should say, a minority even among the whites, who come from every country in Europe but chiefly from Portugal via Madeira. In the census returns a column is headed 'European or Portuguese', a distinction not particularly relished by the Portuguese; they have most of the money in the country, but there are extremely few people in Guiana who are at all rich by European standards.

There are other words peculiar to the colony, many of Dutch or Indian origin; a landing-stage is a 'stelling', a fallen tree, a 'tacuba'; a stream, a 'creek'; a bush path, a 'line'; 'bush' is used for forest as in other parts of the world (I never heard 'jungle' used); open country is 'savannah'; the broad chopping knives used for clearing the lines are called cutlasses; puma and jaguar are called 'tigers'; a halfpenny is a 'cent' and fourpence a 'bit' (this is due to the tiresome currency calculated in dollars and usually worked in pounds and shillings); most curious word of all was that for the blacks who go in little unorganized parties up the rivers to prospect for alluvial gold or diamonds; they are called 'pork knockers' because, it is said, when they are in funds they come into the stores and knock on the counter demanding pork (but this seems as unsatisfactory as most etymological derivations).

Few of the people I talked to had even the most cursory acquaintance with the bush, though most of them could name someone who at one time or another had been up to Kaieteur; they were mostly discouraging and like the books I had read coming out, for quite contradictory reasons; half regarding the expedition as a mild and rather tedious picnic and half as a precipitate and painful suicide. There is always the conviction at the back of people's minds in this part of the world that no stranger can be up to much good, so in order to dispel the suspicion that I was after diamonds, I gave it out, as was indeed the truth, that I wanted to take photographs of the primitive Indians. Here again they were discouraging. 'You'll find them all playing gramophones and working sewing-machines. They're all civilized now. We know what you want,' they said with winks, 'you want to take the girls naked. Well, your best plan is to go up to Bartika and get a few of the tarts there to pose for you. You can get the proper feather ornaments from the Self Help shop. That's what most of the American scientific expeditions do.' Across the Brazilian border I might find something to interest me, but not in Guiana, they said.

I later inquired in more responsible quarters and learned that this was far from being the truth; one whole tribe, the Wei-Weis, still live in absolute seclusion, though the difficulties of reaching these alone were insuperable, but I was to find later, among the Wapishianas, Patamonas and Machusis, people with only the most superficial contact with civilization. But it was all a little discouraging and

23

I realized that though people were anxious enough to help, they could do nothing until I told them what I wanted. I could not just say I wanted to see interesting things because they had no idea what would interest me. It was up to me to fix on a destination and they would tell me how to get there. I had a note of introduction to a Jesuit missionary on the Takutu river and from what I had heard in London about the circumstances of his life, it sounded good enough. There were three Takutu rivers marked on my map, but two were merely guesses, sketched in tentatively with dotted lines, while one was marked firmly as a place of known importance, so I assumed, correctly as it turned out, that this was the one I wanted. It ran through the furthest extremity of the Rupununi savannah forming the boundary between British Guiana and Brazil. Accordingly I made this my objective.

Something should here be said about the history of the Rupununi. It is the only considerable piece of open country in the colony, cut off from the coast by forest and forming, geographically, a part of the big plain which stretches into Brazil beyond the Rio Branco. It was first visited by the explorer Schomburgh in the middle of the last century, claimed vaguely for the British Government with other tracts later ceded to our neighbours, and then left to oblivion until it was rediscovered by a highly romantic character named Mr Melville. This gentleman, who died a few years back, was a parson's son from Jamaica. His story, as told me by one of his daughters, was that after various unsuccessful attempts at gold washing he was found by some Wapishiana Indians dying of fever in the upper Essequibo. He expressed a desire to die in open country and they accordingly carried him to the Rupununi savannah where he made an immediate recovery. The Indians at that time had no trade connection at all with the coast. Melville began bartering in a small way, taking down a yearly boat to Georgetown loaded with hammocks and other examples of Indian workmanship and bringing back fish hooks, axe heads, patent medicines and other desirable commodities. He won the Indians' confidence, married among them, and presently began keeping cattle on a gradually increasing scale until by 1914 he was living in patriarchal authority at a large ranch named Dadanawa.

There was at this time no connection with the coast except by boat down the Essequibo, a journey always arduous, often dangerous and sometimes impossible. His cattle were all sold over the border into Brazil and the country was to all appearance Brazilian; the few other ranchers were Brazilian, Portuguese was the language, there was no representative of government except Melville himself who had been presented with the title of magistrate; there was no attempt to collect customs duties on the trade across the Takutu.

Then with the outbreak of war came a sudden demand for beef. It became necessary to find a way for the Rupununi cattle to reach the Georgetown market. It is impossible to navigate the Essequibo with large boats; the long-debated railway to the interior was no nearer being begun; accordingly it was decided to cut a trail down the already existing Indian line from the beginning of the bush at Anai, to the highest navigable point, Takama, on the Berbice river. The route ran over countless deep creeks; there was no question of making a road for wheeled vehicles but simply a track down which the beasts could be got alive and fattened up again at pasture on the coast. There were numerous, serious objections to the plan, notably the immense leakage through animals accustomed to the savannah, stampeding into the bush from which they could never be recovered, and also through their dying of exhaustion and lack of food on the ten days' drive. However, Melville sold out his whole interests while the scheme was still popular and handed over his huge territory to a newly formed Rupununi Development Company which has carried on a precarious existence ever since. Meanwhile Melville's family still hold complete predominance in the district, all the key positions being held by his sons and sons-in-law.

The cattle trail is one of the chief grumbles of the colony; that and the new road which the present Government is constructing from Bartika to Kaieteur, presumably because these are its chief recent activities and bar politics all over the world consist of grumbling at the Government. In most dependencies I have found that the Public Works Department was the chief butt of conversation; in Guiana it was always the Lands and Mines.

As soon as I decided to make for Takutu I was advised to go and see Bain, the Commissioner for the district, who by good chance was in Georgetown for Christmas. So with the Governor's introduction I sought him out in the boarding-house where he was staying. He was a middle-aged, emaciated man, Creole with some Indian blood. Like everyone else in the colony he had at one time worked gold and diamonds; like most other people he had also been a surveyor, a soldier, a policeman and a magistrate; he had lately returned to the last avocation which included most of the other functions. He received me with great kindness and vivacity, telling me that the Rupununi was the most beautiful place in the world and that anyone with a gift for expression should be able to make a book about it. He was himself returning in a day or two by the cattle trail as far as Kurupukari which was well on my way. He had a boat of stores leaving almost at once from Bartika which he expected to find awaiting him. He offered me a place in that.

'It ought to get there before me,' he said. 'I do not know about the rains. Perhaps it will take four days, perhaps eight. But it must get there because it is full of barbed wire I need. Unless of course it's wrecked,' he added. 'Mr Winter's boat was totally destroyed in the rapids the day before yesterday.'

I had no idea where Kurupukari was, but it sounded as good as anywhere else. When I got back I looked for it on the map. Mr Bain had spoken very quickly so that when I found Yupukarri right up on the savannah I was highly delighted. It was not for two days that I found Kurupukari about a hundred miles away from it. Then I realized that I was in for a longer journey than I had anticipated, and trebled my order for stores.

These were a difficulty, partly because, under the present arrangement, I was to leave before the end of the New Year holidays which meant that I had only one day in which to get everything, but chiefly because I had no idea what I should need. Again opinion was contradictory, some people saying, 'Just take a gun and live by that,' and others, 'Don't count on getting *anything* up country. The ranchers live on *farine*.'

I had no idea what *farine* was but I felt I should need something else. Mr Bain simply said, 'You should be like me. I can go for days without eating – like a camel. That is the way to live in the bush.'

I had already begun to guess that travelling in an empty country was going to be very different from Africa where labour is almost unlimited. It was not a case for luxurious 'chop boxes' of varied delicacies. I realized that moving stores from place to place was going to be a problem – how great a problem I did not know until later. So I concentrated on necessaries – flour, sugar, corned beef, potatoes, rum and so on – bought hammock, gun, mosquito net and blanket, delivered them to the firm who were organizing Mr Bain's boat and settled down to enjoy the last two days in Georgetown.

From that moment onwards I did not have an hour's certainty of plan. It was arranged that I should take Tuesday's steamer to Bartika and start in the boat on Wednesday; then, I discovered by chance that there was no steamer on Tuesdays; wires were sent and the boat delayed until Thursday.

Then Mr Bain rang me to say he was sending a black policeman with me who was to act as my servant; that sounded all right until the agents rang up to say that now the policeman was coming there would only be room for 100 pounds of my stores. There was nothing to do except countermand three-quarters of them.

Then the agents rang up to say, did I realize that it was an open boat and that since the rains were on it was imperative to take a tarpaulin? Desperate and unsuccessful attempts to secure a tarpaulin with every shop in Georgetown closed.

Then Mr Bain rang up to say that the agents said it was an open boat and that the rains were on. I should be soaked to the skin every day and undoubtedly get fever and he could not take the responsibility of sending me in it.

Then I went to see Mr Bain and he said I had better come to Takama with him and perhaps there would be a horse to get me to Kurupukari.

Then I rang up the agents and said that since the boat was relieved of my weight they were to put all my stores on board.

Then Mr Bain rang up to say that he had come to the conclusion that I could have the horse which he had meant to pack with his personal stores; instead he would send them by boat.

Then I rang up the agents and said they were to take from my stores the weight equivalent to the personal stores Mr Bain was sending by boat.

All these, and other less remarkable alarms, occurred at intervals of two or three hours. I may also note that for each telephone call successfully put through there were five or six failures; that I never left the hotel for an hour without finding messages on my return to ring up Mr Bain and the agent urgently; that whenever I rang them up they had just gone out; and that on the last day I was lying in

27

severe pain, poisoned with a local delicacy called 'crab-back' and imagining that I had cholera. Taken all in all it was a disturbed departure.

There was plenty going on in Georgetown that week.

An unknown Dutchman shot himself on Christmas morning in his room at the rival hotel, on account of feeling lonely.

A gentleman known to his friends as 'the Blood of Corruption' was arrested on numerous charges. He was the leader of a criminal organization called 'the Beasts of Berlin'. They had taken the name from a cinema film; none of them had the remotest idea what Berlin was; they just liked the name. But they were perfectly serious criminals for all that.

There was a race-meeting in heavy rain and, on New Year's Eve, a large number of dances. At my hotel there was a Caledonian Ball, characterized by a marked male predominance, pipers and quite elderly men sitting giggling on the ballroom floor; there was also a more decorous function at the club where I ate the poisoned 'crab-back'. There were several 'swizzle parties', an institution which dates from long before the North American cocktail party, starts at six and goes on till midnight. There was a Negro masquerade – an unorganized and more or less spontaneous exhibition of joviality; the gayer spirits dressed up in comic fancy dress and clowned about in Camp Street, each followed by a small court of admirers. There was said to be a 'Komfa' dance (I do not know if that is the right spelling). These dances, the direct descendants of the African 'Ngoma', still takes place from time to time along the coast in out-of-the-way bits of waste ground, usually at the full moon; they are illegal for they usually conclude with an orgy and are apparently associated with voodooism. A young engineer whom I had met on the boat had news of one from one of his workmen. We drove about in search of it for the greater part of one evening but failed to locate it.

Through all this the preparations for the journey up-country, the buying of chlorodyne and bandages, gun caps and cartridge cases, flour and kerosene, seemed fantastic and unsubstantial, and the empty forest, a few miles away, infinitely remote, as unrelated to the crowded life of the coast as it was to London. Most journeys, I think, begin and all end with a sense of unreality. Even when eventually I found myself in the train for New Amsterdam, sitting opposite Mr Bain, with our improbable baggage piled up round us, it still required an effort to convince me that we were on our way.

TWO

It is said that the railway along the Guiana coast is the oldest in the Empire. It runs in pretty, flat country over creeks and canals and through gay, ramshackle villages. The stations still bear the names of the old sugar estates but these are mostly split up now into small holdings growing coconut and rice. The further one goes from Georgetown towards New Amsterdam, the blacker become the inhabitants, of purer Negro type and more cheerful manners. Berbice men look on Demerarans as wasters; the Demerarans look on them as bumpkins.

It was just dark by the time Mr Bain and I reached New Amsterdam. We had the carriage to ourselves and our baggage. Most of the way Mr Bain talked.

I do not know how the legend originated that the men who administer distant territories are 'strong and silent'. It is all against the testimony of observed fact. Some may start strong and even retain a certain wiriness into middle life, but most of them, by the time they have attained any eminence in the King Emperor's service, are subject to one or more severe complaints. As for their silence, it seems to vary in exact inverse ratio to their distance from civilization. For silence one must go to the pie-faced young diners-out of London; men in the wide open spaces are, in my experience, wildly garrulous; many of them, I have noticed, contract the habit of talking to themselves or to dogs and natives, equally ignorant of their language. What is more, they will talk on all subjects – highly personal reminiscences, their dreams, diet and digestion, science, history, morals and theology. But pre-eminently of theology. It seems to be the obsession waiting round the corner for all lonely men. You start talking bawdy with some breezy, rum-drinking tramp skipper and in ten minutes he is proving or disproving the doctrine of original sin.

Mr Bain, though indefatigable in his duty, was not strong; frequent attacks of fever had left him bloodless and fleshless, and besides this he suffered from constant appalling bouts of asthma which kept him awake for all but an hour or two every night. Nor was he silent. During the stimulating fortnight I was to spend in his company he talked at large on every conceivable topic, eagerly, confidently, enthusiastically, not always accurately, sometimes scarcely coherently, inexhaustibly; with inspired imagination, with dizzy changes of thought and rather alarming theatrical effects, in a vocabulary oddly compounded of the jargon he was accustomed to use among his subordinates and the longer, less habitual words he had noticed in print. As I have said he talked of everything at one time or another, but mostly either in metaphysical speculation or in anecdote. He himself always figured prominently in the latter and it was in these that his gestures became most dramatic. The dialogue was all in *oratio recta*; never 'I ordered him to go at once,' but 'I say to him, "Go! plenty quick, quick. Go!"' and at the words Mr Bain's finger would shoot out accusingly, his body would stiffen and quiver, his eyes would blaze until I began to fear he would induce some kind of seizure.

One engaging and lamentably uncommon trait in Mr Bain's reminiscences was this, that besides, like half the world, remembering and retailing all the injustices he had encountered, he also remembered and retained every word of approbation; the affection he had received from his parents as a boy; the prize given to him at school for his geometry; the high commendation he had had at the technical college for his draughtsmanship; numberless spontaneous expressions of esteem from various acquaintances throughout his life, the devotion of subordinates and the confidence of superiors; the pleasure the Governor took in his official reports; testimonies from delinquents to the impartiality, mercy, and wisdom of his judicial sentences – all these were fresh and glowing in his memory and all or nearly all, I was privileged to hear.

Many of his stories I found to strain the normal limits of credulity – such as that he had a horse which swam under water and a guide who employed a parrot to bring him information; the bird would fly on ahead, said Mr Bain, and coming back to its perch on the Indian's shoulder whisper in his ear what he had seen, who was on the road and where they could find water. I do not think that there was any conscious effort to deceive. I think that like many raconteurs he drew no clear distinction between what had actually occurred and what he had told a fair number of times as a good story. But most people dislike the idea that they are having their legs pulled and I soon fell into what now seems to me an ungenerous and exasperating habit of cross-examination, which usually disinterred some closely concealed nucleus of verbal truth.

At sundown it became cold and clammy in the carriage; clouds of mosquitoes came in from windows and corridor, biting us to frenzy. Mr Bain remarked gloomily that they were probably all infected with malaria. Everyone has different theories about quinine; Mr Bain recommended constant, large doses, observing parenthetically that they caused deafness, insomnia and impotence.

We transferred from the train to a ferry steamer and drifted rather disconsolately across to the town. There was a boarding-house kept by a white gentleman in reduced circumstances; here we dined in a swarm of mosquitoes; the house had run out of drink during the New Year celebrations. After dinner to avoid the mosquitoes we walked about the streets for an hour. They were empty and ill-lit. New Amsterdam, eighty years ago, was a prosperous, if sleepy, town with a club and its own society; now there is barely a handful of whites quartered there, the rest having been driven out by mosquitoes and the decay of the sugar trade. At a street corner we met a Jordanite haranguing a few apathetic loafers and a single suspicious policeman. He wore a long white robe and a white turban and he waved a wand of metal tubing; a drowsy little boy sat beside him holding a large Bible. The Jordanites are one of the many queer sects that flourish among Negroes. They derive their name not as might be supposed from the river, but from a recently deceased Mr Jordan from Jamaica; their object seemed partially pious, partially political; they are said to favour polygamy. The present speaker ran round in little circles as he spoke, 'What for you black men afraid ob de white man? Why you ascared ob his pale face and blue eye? Why do you fear his yellow hair? Because you are all fornicators – dat is de reason. If you were pure of heart you need not fear de white man.'

32

Then he saw us and seemed rather embarrassed. ''Nother text, boy.' But the boy was asleep over the Bible. He cracked him sharply on the head with his wand and the child hastily read a verse of Ezekiel and the preacher took up on another subject.

'The black man got a very inferior complex,' remarked Mr Bain as we resumed our walk.

Next day we started at dawn. There was a great rainbow over the town. On the way to the quay I noticed a charming old Lutheran church, relic of the Dutch occupation, that had been invisible the night before.

A lazy uneventful day in the paddle steamer up the Berbice river. Monotonous vegetable walls on either bank, occasionally broken by bovianders' cabins.† Now and then an unstable dug-out canoe would shoot out from the green shadows and an unkempt, bearded figure would deliver or receive a parcel of mail. We slung our hammocks on deck. There was a steward who made gin-swizzles of a kind and served revolting meals at intervals of two hours. On the whole a tolerable day's journey.

Our only companions on the top deck were a Belgian rancher, his Indian wife, some of their children, and his wife's sister. They were the first Indians I had seen. Since they had taken up with a European they wore hats and stockings and high-heeled shoes, but they were very shy, guarding their eyes like nuns, and giggling foolishly when spoken to; they had squat little figures and blank, mongol faces. They had bought a gramophone and a few records in town which kept them happy for the twelve hours we were together. Conversation was all between Mr Bain and the rancher, and mostly about horses. I never approach any new horse (and few familiar ones for that matter) without some sinking in self-esteem, so I listened with more than polite interest. Quite different standards of quality seemed to be observed here from those I used to learn from Captain Hance.

'I tell you, Mr Bain, that buckskin of mine was the finest mare bred in this district. You didn't have to use no spur or whip to her. Why before you was on her back, almost, she was off like the wind

---

† Boviander is the name given to the people of unpredictable descent – mostly Dutch, Indian and Negro mixtures – who live in isolated huts all along the lower waters of the big rivers; they generally have a minute clearing where they grow manioc or maize; they fish, and spend most of their time, like the water rat in *Wind in the Willows* 'messing about in boats'.

and *nothing* would stop her. And if she didn't want to go any particular way *nothing* would make her. Why I've been carried six miles out of my course many a time, pulling at her with all my strength. *And* how she could rear.'

'Yes, she *could rear*,' said Mr Bain in wistful admiration. 'It was lovely to see her.'

'And if she got you down she'd roll on you. She wouldn't get up till she'd broken every bone in your body. She killed one of my boys that way.'

'But what about my Tiger?'

'Ah, he was a good horse. You could see by the way he rolled his eyes.'

'Did you ever see him *buck*? Why he'd buck all over the corral. And he was wicked too. He struck out at you if he got a chance.'

'That was a *good* horse, Tiger. What became of him?'

'Broke his back. He bolted over some rocks into a creek with one of the boys riding him.'

'Still you know I think that for *bucking* my Shark . . .'

And so it went on. Presently I asked in some apprehension, 'And the horse I am to ride tomorrow. Is he a *good* horse too?'

'One of the strongest in the country,' said Mr Bain. 'It will be just like the English Grand National for you.'

So the day wore on. The steward trotted about with frightful helpings of curried fish; later with greyish tea and seed cake; later with more fish and lumps of hard, dark beef. The Indian ladies played their gramophone. The rancher had a nap. Mr Bain told me more. At last, about seven, we arrived at our destination, and descended in the dark into a dug-out canoe.

'Be careful, be careful, if you're not used to them you will certainly be drowned,' Mr Bain admonished me, thus giving the first evidence of what, for the next few days, was going to prove a somewhat tiresome solicitude for my safety. The trouble was this. The Governor had requested Mr Bain to look after me and, in his kindness, had stressed the fact that the conditions of the country were new to me and that he took a personal interest in my welfare. Mr Bain, in his kindness, interpreted this to mean that something very precious and very fragile had been put into his charge; if any accident were to befall me the Governor would never forgive it; danger, for one of

34

delicate constitution, lurked in every activity of the day. If I helped to saddle the placid pack ox he would cry out, 'Stand back, be careful, or he will kick out your brains.' If I picked up my own gun he would say, 'Be careful, it will go off and shoot you.'

Fortunately this scrupulous concern began to wear thin after three days' travel, but during those three days it came as near as anything could to straining my affection and gratitude towards him.

The dug-out paddled by an indiscernible figure in the stern, swept away from the ship across the dark water; the opposite bank was lightless. We scrambled up the slippery bank (Mr Bain urging me anxiously not to fall down) and could just make out a rise in the ground surmounted by some kind of building; the boatman brought up a lantern and we climbed further. Mr Bain in the meantime asking fretfully, 'Yetto? Where's Yetto? I told him to be here with my hammock.'

'Yetto come with de horses this morning. Now him go bottom-side to a party. Him no say nothing about de hammock.'

'Yetto proper bad man,' said Mr Bain lapsing into vernacular. 'Him proper Congo.'

Thus in circumstances of discredit and terms of opprobrium I first heard the name of someone to whom I was later to become warmly attached.

We climbed the little hill and reached a thatched shelter, open at the sides, where two figures lay asleep in hammocks. They woke up, sat up and stared at us. A black man and his wife. Mr Bain asked them if they knew what Yetto had done with his hammock.

'Him gone to de party.'

'Where dis party?'

'Down to de river. Indian house. All de boys at de party.'

So we went down to look for Yetto. We paddled almost noiselessly down stream, keeping into the bank. It was an effort to balance in the narrow, shallow craft. Eventually we heard music and hauled in under the bushes.

The party was in a large Indian hut. It was cosmopolitan in character, being made up of Brazilian *vaqueiros* (cowboys), bovianders, blacks and a number of clothed and semi-civilized Indians. Two Brazilians were playing guitars. The hostess came out to greet us.

'Good night,' she said, shaking hands and leading us in. It was not etiquette to ask for Yetto at once so we sat on a bench and waited. A girl was walking from guest to guest with a bowl of dark home-brewed liquor; she handed a mug to each in turn, waiting, while they drank and then refilling it for the next. Two or three Negroes were dancing. The Indians sat in stolid rows, silently, soft hats pulled down over their eyes, staring gloomily at the floor. Now and then one would get up, stroll apathetically across to a girl and invite her to dance. The couple would then shuffle round in a somewhat European manner, separate without a word or a glance and resume their seats. The Indians, I learned later, are a solitary people and it takes many hours' heavy drinking to arouse any social interests in them. In fact the more I saw of Indians the greater I was struck by their similarity to the English. They like living with their own families at great distances from their neighbours; they regard strangers with suspicion and despair; they are unprogressive and unambitious, fond of pets, hunting and fishing; they are undemonstrative in love, unwarlike, morbidly modest; their chief aim seems to be on all occasions to render themselves inconspicuous; in all points, except their love of strong drink and perhaps their improvidence, the direct opposite of the Negro. On this particular evening, however, their only outstanding characteristic was inability to make a party go.

After a time Yetto was detected drinking guiltily in a corner. He was a large middle-aged black of unusual ugliness. He was not ugly in the way a handsome Negro is ugly. He was comic; huge feet and hands, huge mouth, and an absurd little Hitler moustache. He talked with a breadth of Creole intonation that for the first few days was quite unintelligible to me. Mr Bain and he talked at some length about the hammock; a conversation in which 'you proper Congo' occurred frequently. Then he left the party and came away with us to find it. At last at about ten o'clock Mr Bain and I were established in the rest house.

Sleep was not easy. A hammock is one of the most agreeable things for an hour's rest, but it needs practice to adapt it for a night, particularly when it is tied to the same framework as three others, whose occupants with every movement set it vibrating. The hammocks used in Guiana are all of Indian manufacture, woven in thick cotton threads; they are light enough to roll up and tie behind one's saddle and have the particular property that they wrap round the body and 'give' at any change of position. They are so much the cleanest and most portable sort of bed that I wonder they are not more used in other parts of the world. But they take some getting used to. It is not difficult to fall out of them, they are extremely draughty and if you do go to sleep in the wrong position you are liable to wake up stiff in the back. Later I learned the correct way to lie, diagonally instead of vertically; later too I had harder days behind me. On this particular night I slept little. Nor did poor Mr Bain who sat hour after hour with his head between his knees, gasping for breath in the throes of asthma. The black couple, however, made up for us both with enormous rhythmic snores.

Next morning Yetto and some other boys appeared with the horses and the misgivings which I had been suffering ever since the conversation of the previous day rapidly subsided. They were some very small ponies and they stood placidly in the corner of the corral cropping the tops off the arid tufts of grass; they were too lethargic even to switch away the horse flies that clustered on their quarters; mine had been attacked by a vampire bat during the night and bore a slaver of blood on his withers. I never rode a good horse all the time I was on the savannahs; partly, of course, because in no quarter of the globe do people readily lend or hire good horses to a stranger, but chiefly because there are very few of them. Most of the ranches own large herds which are loosed at grass for three quarters of the year. When some are needed the *vaqueiros* are sent out to lasso them and bring them in; they are ridden for a week or two until they begin to show signs of collapse (through the heat of the climate and the cut of the Brazilian saddles they are very easily galled) and then turned out again. They are nearly all promiscuously bred, unshod and grass-fed. Generally, when first in from the savannah, they bucked a little, shied, and were a nuisance for half an hour; after that they settled down to the regular four-mile-an-hour jog-trot; after the fourth hour they had to be spurred and whipped to keep them in motion at all.

Mr Bain had various duties to occupy him; the packing of the ox took some care, and it was noon before we were ready. The black man, who had shared the rest house the night before, was coming with us. He was manager of the ranch ten or twelve miles away, which was to be our first stop. We mounted and made to start off. My pony would not move.

'Loosen de reins,' they said.

I loosened the reins and kicked him and hit. He took a few steps backwards.

'Loosen de reins,' they said.

Then I saw how they were riding, with the reins hanging quite loose, their hands folded on the front of the saddle. That is the style all over this part of the world; the reins are never tightened except in an occasional savage jerk; the aids are given on the neck instead of on the bit. Drama in movement is the object aimed at; the *vaqueiros* like a horse that as soon as they mount him will give two or three leaps in the air and then start off at a gallop; it does not matter how short a time the gallop lasts provided he takes them out of sight of the spectator; then after many hours' monotonous jogging they will spur him into life when they approach either ranch or village, arrive at the gallop, the horse's mouth lathered with foam, rein him back on to his hocks and dismount in a small dust storm. I had seen this often enough in the old days of the cinema, but had not realized that it occurred in real life.

We set off across the plain, cantering a little but mostly jogging at what for many weeks was to be my normal travelling gait. The country was dead flat and featureless except for ant-hills and occasional clumps of palm; the ground was hard earth and sand tufted with dun-coloured grass; thousands of lizards scattered and darted under the horses' feet; otherwise there was no sign of life except the black crows who rose at our approach from the carcasses strewn along the track, and resettled to their feast behind us. Here and in the forest we passed a carcass every half-mile. Many were recently dead, for the last drive had lost 40 per cent, and these we cantered past holding our breath; others were mere heaps of bone picked white by the ants, the mound of half-digested feed always prominent among the ribs.

During the ride Mr Bain discoursed to the black rancher about history; I listened fitfully for my horse was continually dropping behind, but I was never out of earshot of the voice, voluble, rhapsodic, now rising to some sharp catastrophe, now running on evenly, urgently, irresistibly in the shimmering noon heat.

I caught bits '... once, you see, there was nothing but water. It says so in the Bible. Water covered the face of the earth. Then He divided the land from the waters. How did He do that, Mr Yerwood? Why, by killing de crabs, and all de shells of de crabs became ground down by the tides and became sand . . .'

' . . . then there was Napoleon. He was only a little corporal but he divorced his wife and married the daughter of an Emperor. Mark my words, Mr Yerwood, all dose Bolshevists will be doing that soon . . .'

' . . . and why did the English take so long to subdue de little Boers? Because dey were so sporting. When dey take prisoners dey let dem go again for to give dem another chance . . .'

We reached our destination in about two hours and found three sheds and a wired corral. It was less than I had expected. Through the influence of the cinema, 'ranch' had taken on a rather glorious connotation in my mind; of solid, whitewashed buildings; a court-yard with a great tree casting its shadow in the centre and a balustraded wall, wrought iron gates, a shady interior with old Spanish furniture and a lamp burning before a baroque Madonna, and lovely girls with stock-whips and guitars. I do not say that I had expected to find this at Waranana; in fact it would have greatly surprised me; but I did feel that the word 'ranch' had taken a fall.

Various dependants of Mr Bain's were awaiting him here – policemen returning to duty, woodmen in charge of keeping the trail open; he also had stores and saddlery and some horses, left behind on his previous journey. All these he attended to so that by next morning everything was ready for us to start out. A moody young policeman named Price was handed over to me (or me to him), to act as my personal servant. Yetto was never far away, grinning sheepishly and constantly reprimanded. He held an uncer-tain position, partly government runner, partly groom, partly cook, partly porter.

Mr Yerwood killed a chicken for us and, after we had dined, joined us and drank some of our rum. He and Mr Bain talked about animals, their stories growing less probable as the evening progressed. Finally Mr Yerwood described a 'water-monkey' he had once seen; it was enormous and jet black; it had a grinning mouth full of sharp teeth; it swam at a great speed; its habit was to submerge itself and wait for bathers whom it would draw down and pound to pieces on the rocks at the bottom. Just such an occurrence had happened to a friend of Mr Yerwood's; every bone in his body was broken when it floated to the surface, Mr Yerwood said.

Not to be outdone, Mr Bain related how once, when walking in the late afternoon in the neighbourhood of Mount Roraima, he had encountered two Missing Links, a man and his wife slightly over normal size but bowed and simian in their movements; they were naked except for a light covering of soft reddish down; they had stared at Mr Bain a full half-minute, then said something he did not understand and strolled off into the bush. After that there was little to be said on the subject of animals. It was ten o'clock – late for the district – so we took to our hammocks, leaving the lamp burning as a protection against vampire bats.

It would be tedious to record the daily details of the journey to Kurupukari. Mr Bain managed everything; I merely trotted beside him; we took six days from the ranch, averaging about fifteen miles a day. Mr Bain often explained how, in normal conditions, he did the whole journey in two stages at full gallop all the way. On this occasion we had to keep pace with the pack oxen and the walking men, and anyway I do not think our ponies were up to much more. All the time we only passed one human being – a Portuguese-speaking Indian, padding along on foot, going down to the river on some inscrutable errand. For two days we travelled over grass land and then entered the bush on crossing the Yawakuri river. Immediately our entire conditions changed; it was cool and quite sunless. The green, submarine darkness of the jungle has been described frequently enough but it can never, I think, be realized until one has been there. The trail was as broad as an English lane with vast, impenetrable walls of forest rising to a hundred and fifty feet on either side; the first twenty feet from the ground were dense undergrowth, then the trunks of the trees emerged, quite bare, like architectural columns rising vertical and featureless until they broke into the solid roof of leaves, through which appeared only rare star points of direct sunlight. There were always men working to keep the trail clear of fallen timber and there were always trees lying across it at frequent intervals. Usually some kind of line had been chopped round these through the bush and we would dismount and lead our horses. There were also creeks every few miles, low at this time of year, so that we could ride through them. In the wet season,

Mr Bain said, you had to crawl across a tacuba leading a swimming horse, carry your baggage across and load and reload your pack animals four or five times a day. Sometimes the trail had been completely cleared with a 'corduroy' of logs through the marshy places; elsewhere only the undergrowth had been chopped away and the trees stood up in the middle of the path; once we came to a place where the virgin forest had been burned and a second growth of low bush had taken its place; there was loose white sand here, blinding to the eyes after the gloom of the forest and heavy going for the horses.

Everyone who has ever been there has remarked on the apparent emptiness of the bush. The real life, so naturalists write, takes place a hundred feet up in the tree-tops; it is there that you would find all the flowers and parrots and monkeys, high overhead in the sunlight, never coming down except when there is a storm. Occasionally we would find the floor of the trail strewn with petals from flowers out of sight above us. I have not a naturalist's trained observation and no doubt missed many things that he would have seen; certainly I saw little enough; one jaguar slinking away ahead of us, two or three acouris, a large rodent that makes possible but dull eating, some tortoises that the boys eagerly collected for meat, an incredible number of ants; ants of all sizes and shades, alone and in endless caravans; they were everywhere; it was impossible to find a square three inches of ground anywhere without an ant in it; you could not throw away the dregs of your mug without drowning one.

We met the first snake on our first day in the bush. Mr Bain and I were riding abreast a mile or so ahead of the baggage. He was telling me his views on marriage ('. . . whom God has joined together let no man put asunder. Yes. But tell me this. Who is God? God is love. So when a couple have ceased to love one another . . .') when he suddenly reined up and said in a melodramatic whisper: 'Stop. Look ahead. Dere is a terrible great snake.' It was in the days when he still regarded my safety as peculiarly precarious. 'Don't come near – it may attack you.'

Sure enough, about twenty yards ahead was a very large snake, curled up in the middle of the trail.

'What kind is it?'

'I never saw anything like him before. Look at his terrible great head,' hissed Mr Bain.

It certainly was a very odd-looking head from where we sat, swollen and brown and quite different in appearance from the mottled coils. Mr Bain dismounted and I followed. Very stealthily, step by step he approached the creature. It did not move and so, emboldened, he began to throw pieces of dead wood at it. None of them fell within six feet of their mark. He approached closer, motioning me back apprehensively. Then the snake suddenly raised his neck, retched and for a moment it appeared as though his head had fallen off. Then it became clear what had happened. We had surprised a python in the act of slowly swallowing a large toad. It had got down the back legs and was slowly sucking in the body when it had been disturbed; the 'terrible great head' was the toad's body half in and half out of the jaws. The python averted its own delicately pointed face and slipped away into the bush; the toad showed little gratitude or surprise at his escape, but dragged himself rather laboriously under a log and sat down to consider his experience.

But if there was little to see there was a great deal to hear; always, but particularly from sunset until dawn, the bush was alive with sounds. We used to turn in early, usually between seven and eight, because there was nothing to do after dark; there were no chairs to sit in or table to sit at; the lantern light was too dim for reading. As soon as we finished supper we rolled up in our hammocks and there was nothing to do but lie and listen for ten or eleven hours. There were the immediate sounds of poor Mr Bain's asthma; of the boys squatting round their fire, sometimes singing, more often arguing, always quite unintelligible when they were among themselves; there were our own beasts grazing in the corral and limping about at hobble; often we would hear the crash of dead timber falling in the forest near us, but around and above and through all these were the sounds of the bush. As I have said, I am no naturalist; Mr Bain's experienced ear was able to pick out innumerable voices that to me were merged in the general chatter, but even to me there were some sounds that were unmistakable; there were the 'howler' monkeys; I never saw one except stuffed in a museum – he was a small ginger creature – but we heard them roaring like lions most days; in the far distance it was like the noise of the dredgers that once used to attend me lying sleepless night after night at Port Said. There were the frogs, some shrill like those in the South of France, others deep and hoarse. There was a bird which mooed like a cow, named, appositely enough, the 'cow-bird', and another which struck two sharp metallic notes as though with a hammer on a copper cistern; this was called the 'bell-bird'; there was a bird that made a noise like a motor bicycle starting up; a kind of woodpecker drilling very rapidly with his beak; there were others of various kinds who whistled like errand boys. There was one which repeated '*Qu'est ce qu'il dit?*' endlessly in a challenging tone. There was one insect which buzzed in a particular manner. 'Listen,' said Mr Bain one day, 'that is most interesting. It is what we call the "six o'clock beetle", because he always makes that noise at exactly six o'clock.'

'But it is now quarter past four.'

'Yes, that is what is so interesting.'

At one time and another in the country I heard the 'six o'clock beetle' at every hour of the day and night.

But experienced 'bush men' say that they can tell the time as accurately by the sounds of the bush, as a mariner can by the sun.

On the whole this part of the journey was comfortable enough. We had ample stores; every evening there was a creek to wash in; nothing went seriously wrong with the animals or the boys; there was no rain. At night we lay in the rest houses that have been put up every fifteen miles or so for the *vaqueiros* driving down the cattle. These are simply thatched shelters, sometimes with floors and breast-high walls; there was no furniture and sometimes we found the fabric of the place half demolished by bucks who, with their peculiar improvidence, had chopped it up for firewood rather than step five yards to the bush outside; often too we found the houses foul with the remains of bad fish and meat left by the previous occupants; once a cow had died to windward of us whom it had been no one's business to remove. Yetto's cooking was unbelievable and consisted mainly of boiling up corned beef with vast quantities of red peppers and rock salt. But, as I have said it was on the whole a comfortable week and a delightful one. There was enough exertion to make one glad when one had reached the day's destination; the new scenery, utterly unlike anything I had seen before, was a continual pleasure. Mr Bain's company was a full enough experience in itself. When on the seventh day we reached Kurupukari I was sorry that this stage of the journey was over.

Kurupukari was marked large on the map and had figured constantly in our conversation for the past week. I had little idea, however, of what to expect and vaguely imagined something like the lake stations at Victoria Nyanza or Lake Tanganyika – a pier, a government office, the Commissioner's residence, half a dozen corrugated iron store-houses, a shop or two, a post office, a handful of native huts and a flagstaff. What I found was a surprise. There was a flagstaff, certainly, lying flat in the grass, still under construction; it was completed and erected during my stay; later Mr Bain hopes to obtain a flag for it. But there was no landing, no habitations, only a single wooden house standing in a clearing on a slight hill.

The Essequibo bends there, so that the place had the look of a peninsula; the river even at this season was immense, and the wooden islands round which it divided and converged made it seem larger still; a broad creek flowed into it immediately opposite the station; there were sand dunes and rocks, submerged at full flood, but now high and dry, confusing one's sense of direction; there were cascades and patches of still lake so that one seemed to be surrounded by a system of ornamental waters, and across its vast and varied expanse one could see the green precipices of forest and appreciate, as one could not when directly beneath them, the freakish height of the trees and the gay dapple of blossom at their summit.

The house, like most in the country, was of one storey, raised on piles ten or twelve feet from the ground. There were steps leading to a verandah; in the interior was a single, large room, with partitioned cubicles at the sides. This room was the law court, dignified with a dais, a witness stand and a dock; in one of the cubicles was an iron bedstead which I occupied, the others had struts for the hammocks; the verandah was the living-room with a table and two armchairs. It was also the government office; some tattered, printed regulations, a calendar and an obsolete map hung on the walls; there was a desk with pigeon-holes for licences, forms, stamps; here were transacted the multifarious functions of local government; a tax was levied on passing cattle, grants of land were registered, pilots' certificates were endorsed, letters were accepted for the irregular river service to the coast. A resident black sergeant of police took charge of them. Under us, between the supporting piles, there lived, under the minimum of restraint, a dozen or so convicts. These were mostly Indians serving sentence for cattle stealing; they were sent out daily to work on the trail armed with cutlasses, under the supervision of a single policeman or under no supervision at all; they were sometimes sent as messengers on two- or three-day journeys alone into the bush; they slept under a more solid shelter than in their homes and ate more regularly and more copiously and all returned the fatter and prouder for their contact with civilization.

Mr Bain's cubicle had a cupboard, without lock, in which he kept or attempted to keep, a few personal possessions; on the walls were pasted some pictures of film stars cut out of magazines and a few picture postcards. Any passing rancher would and constantly did, occupy the room, for the house was a regular rest house on the trail and it was usually a matter of a day or so to get a drive across the river (once there had been a flat-bottomed ferry boat to facilitate the operation but that had lately been sunk and the last few drives had had to swim across with deplorable losses). Everyone in fact who passed on any occasion used the house as a matter of right; the captains and bosuns of the river boats squatted about chatting in the courtroom, bucks in for a gun licence spent a day or two getting the latest river gossip; ballata† collectors waited here for transport. This busy place was the nearest thing Mr Bain had to a home, a curious contrast to the trim little official residences of British Africa. In all his huge district there was not one place which Mr Bain could lock up; his life was spent eternally jogging up and down the cattle trail and across the plain to the ultimate frontier station at Bon Success, hanging his hammock in the *vaqueiros'* shelters or putting up the night at the scattered little ranch houses of the savannah, living from year's end to year's end in camp conditions except for rare official visits to a Georgetown boarding-house. It was not everybody's job.

Unsatisfactory news awaited us at Kurupukari; our boat from Bartika had not arrived and Mr Bain, who had hitherto been unreasonably confident about it, suddenly became correspondingly depressing. That was the way in the bush, he said, one had to be used to things like that; there was not much water in the river, no doubt they were having a difficult time at the rapids; it might be weeks before they arrived; they might never arrive at all; that was

---

† A substitute for rubber used principally for submarine cables; periodically a thriving trade product in the forest. The Indians bleed it from trees, and exchange it with representatives of a local company for cloth, hardware, etc.

probably it – the boat had been wrecked and the men all drowned; the barbed wire and the stores anyway would be lost beyond hope. How right he had been to bring me up the trail ... and so on.

Meanwhile we were reduced to the milder discomforts of a state of siege; of a siege in the early days, that is to say, before the garrison get properly down to eating their own wounded. We had a box and a half of biscuits and a tin of milk; otherwise we had exhausted all our tinned stores. We were entirely out of butter, potatoes, flour, sugar, rum and tobacco. It was uncomfortable, particularly as there seemed no certainty of relief, but there was no danger of starvation. There were several bullocks grazing outside the house, one of which Mr Bain had killed and dried; a boviander across the water grew a little maize; and there were great sacks of *farine* for the convicts' rations. Both this and the dried beef need a word or two of explanation, since they are the staple diet of the cattle country and less palatable or satisfying food I never struck in any part of the world.

Farine is a vegetable product made from cassava root. It is tantalizing to speculate how it ever came to be discovered, for cassava in its natural state is poisonous and a fairly elaborate process of pulping and squeezing and drying is necessary to convert it to an edible condition. When and how, in the unchronicled days before the first European explorers of the sixteenth century, did the Indians conceive the idea? After what failures and experiments? How did the taste and knowledge spread among the countless antagonistic nationalities? For over a great part of the continent, among tribes utterly dissimilar in race and habit are found the same cultivated cassava crops, the same ingenious wicker tubes that contract and expand in its manufacture. There seems no answer to this or to the other more immediate question; why, now that most parts are comparatively accessible and other cereals can be introduced, do not only the Indians but the foreign settlers persist in planting this one vegetable that takes most trouble to prepare and is most repulsive when prepared? I asked several people and they said vaguely that it was the food of the country; that the boys expected it; that one got used to it in time. For I used 'edible' in the same sense as it is used in the bush as qualifying any substance not actively lethal; turtles' eggs are considered 'edible', so are lizards and the fat white grubs which inhabit the heart of some palm trees; on the way up Mr Bain would frequently offer me bitter little berries or tasteless, mushy

46

fruits as 'bush food'. *Farine* was very difficult to manage. It is like coarse sawdust in appearance; a granulated, tapioca-coloured substance of intense hardness and a faint taste of brown paper. It is eaten quite alone, or with hot water to soften it or more luxuriously with milk or the water in which the *tasso* has been boiled.

Tasso is the dry beef mentioned above. It is the incarnation of every joke ever made about meat at schools or messes or charitable institutions. It would certainly cause a mutiny in any English prison. It is prepared in this way. The killing of a beast is an event of some importance in the immediate neighbourhood. Indians get news of it and appear mysteriously like gulls round a trawler when the catch is cleaned. A few choice morsels are cut away and cooked and eaten fresh. The Indians carry off the head and the entrails. The rest is sliced into thin slabs, rolled in salt and hung up to dry. A few days of sun and hot savannah wind reduce it to a black, leathery condition in which it will remain uncorrupt indefinitely. Even the normally omnivorous ants will not touch it. It is rolled up and tied to the back of one's saddle; it is even, so I was told, put under the saddle above the blanket to keep it tender and protect the horse from galling. When the time comes to eat it, it is scrubbed fairly clean of dust and salt and boiled in water. It emerges softened but fibrous and tasteless. I can conceive it might be possible for a newcomer to stomach a little *farine* with a rich and aromatic stew; or a little *tasso* with plenty of fresh vegetables and bread. The food of the savannah is *farine* and *tasso* and nothing else.

For four days there was no sign of the boat. I went out with a gun but did not see any game. It had all migrated, Mr Bain said, on account of the dry weather and the boviander's hunting. Lack of tobacco was making us short of temper. There seemed no point in hanging on indefinitely; if the boat had been sunk we should not hear news of it for weeks. I decided to take some *tasso* and biscuits and set off for Annai at the end of the cattle trail, where the resident policeman was said to keep hens. From him I could get enough provisions to take me to the first ranch and so move on by stages to Bon Success where there was a Portuguese store. From there it was only a few miles to the mission house. Mr Bain could lend me a riding horse and a pack horse as far as Annai, and Yetto all the way. A policeman was also going up to duty at Bon Success who would carry a certain amount of baggage. It would be a far less comfortable

47

journey than the first week had been, but it was possible. Anything was better than staying on without books or provisions at Kurupu-kari. Then when all this was decided, late on the last afternoon, one of the convicts reported the sound of a motor. Mr Bain and I hurried down to the river bank. He too could hear it plainly, though it was half an hour before a sound reached my duller ears. Pessimistic to the last, Mr Bain said it was probably some other boat, but in the end, just at sundown it came into sight, a grey blob very slowly approaching. Their sharper eyes – Mr Bain's and the little cluster of convicts and police – instantly recognized it as ours. In another half-hour it was there. An open boat low in the water, with an outboard engine. Nothing could be unloaded that night. There was a crew of four or five, each with a story to tell. They camped near the boat and long into the night we could hear them arguing and boasting over their fire. We went to bed suffused as though by wine with renewed geniality.

The unloading took all the morning and as I saw my stores packed bit by bit against the wall of my cubicle I began to despair of ever moving them. But Yetto was confident that he and the horse and the policeman could manage them with ease. We swam the horses across the river that afternoon and hobbled them in the corral on the opposite bank so that they would be ready to start the next day. The pack horse took unkindly to the water and swallowed a good deal on the way across.

Everything seemed set for my departure. I had even some kind of plan evolved for my ultimate route. It was possible, said Mr Bain, to take a canoe from Bon Success down the Takutu to Boa Vista. That meant nothing to me but Mr Bain explained that it was an important Brazilian town – next to Manaos the most important town in Amazonas. He had never been there himself but he knew those who had and in his description he made it a place of peculiar glamour – dissipated and violent; a place where revolutions were plotted and political assassinations committed; from there regular paddle steamers plied to Manaos – a city of inexpressible grandeur, of palaces and opera houses, boulevards and fountains, swaggering military in spurs and white gloves, cardinals and millionaires; and from there great liners went direct to Lisbon. Mr Bain made a very splendid picture of it all – so graphic and full of passages so personal and penetrating that it was difficult to accept his assurance that he knew it only by repute. His eyes flashed as he told me of it and his arms swept in circles. I felt that it was a singularly fortunate man who went to Boa Vista and Manoas.

On the eve of my departure Mr Bain and I had an intimate and convivial dinner. Next morning I sent the stores across with Yetto and the policeman; they were to arrange the pack horse's load and their own and start ahead of me. Soon after midday I went across myself. Mr Bain came to see me off. We found and saddled the horse; I mounted and after many expressions of mutual good will, I rode off alone up the trail.

THREE

As soon as I set out on my own, things began to go slightly against
me; I was pursued by no cataclysmic doom but by a series of mild
mishaps which began within half an hour of my saying goodbye to
Mr Bain.

I was jogging happily up the trail, feeling for the first time a little
like an explorer, when I met the neighbouring boviander squatting
moodily on a tree stump beside a pile of tins that were obviously
part of my stores. The man grinned amiably and took off his hat.
'Yetto and Price say to take dese back,' he explained. 'Horse no can
carry. Him lie down all de time.'

'Lies down?'

'All de time. Dey beat him with a stick and him goes little little
way and den him lie down again. Him no get top-side. De boys
make pack lighter.'

I looked at the pile and saw that with a minimum of discrimi-
nation, they had abandoned my entire meat ration. There seemed
nothing to be done. I picked out half a dozen tins, rolled them up
in the hammock at the back of my saddle and told the man to present
the rest to Mr Bain with my compliments. Then I rode on less
contentedly.

About six miles farther on I came upon the pack horse unsaddled
and hobbled, his pack lying on the ground near him. I shouted for
Yetto who eventually appeared from the bush where he and Price
had been having a nap.

'Him weary,' said Yetto. 'Him no carry pack top-side.' We undid
the loads and rearranged them, sifting out everything unessential
from the heap. An Indian boy had appeared mysteriously and I

entrusted to him the stores we could not take, to carry back to Kurupukari. Then I rode on ahead to the shelter where we should spend the night. I waited two hours and there was no trace of the baggage. Then I resaddled my horse and rode back. About a mile from where I had left them, Yetto and Price were sitting on a fallen tree eating *farine*. The horse was grazing near them, the packs were on the ground.

'Dat horse am sick. Him no go at all.'

It was now late afternoon. There was nothing for it but to return to Kurupukari, so I left Price to guard the stores, told Yetto to follow with the pack horse and rode back again to the river.

That ride remains one of the most vivid memories of the cattle trail. Checked and annoyed as I was, the splendour of the evening compensated for everything. Out on the savannah there is no twilight; the sun goes down blazing on the horizon, affording five or ten minutes of gold and crimson glory; then darkness. In the forest night opens slowly like a yawn. The colours gradually deepened, the greens pure and intense to the point of saturation, the tree trunks and the bare earth glowing brown; the half shades, the broken and refracted fragments of light all disappeared and left only fathomless depths of pure colour. Then dusk spread; distance became incalculable and obstacles detached themselves unexpectedly and came suddenly near; and while it was almost night in the trail the tops of the trees were still ablaze with sunlight, till eventually they too darkened and their flowers were lost. And all the pattering and whistling and chattering of the bush at night broke out loudly on all sides, and the tired little horse – who was doing a double journey and, being always on the move, had no instinct for home – suddenly pricked his ears and raised his head and stepped out fresh as though his day were only just beginning.

It was black night when I reached the corral. I hobbled him, took off his bridle and saddle and carried them down to the water's edge. The other bank showed no light. After prolonged shouting I heard an answering call and twenty minutes later a canoe appeared suddenly at my feet. We paddled to the house and I sent the man reluctantly back for Yetto. Mr Bain received me without surprise. He never thought I would get far alone.

Next day there was more reorganization. The pack horse was clearly unfit for the journey so the sergeant hired me a donkey

51

named Maria and a vain young Negro named Sinclair, who had been hanging about without apparent purpose in and out of the house for some days. I was still obliged to abandon a great part of my stores. One of the heaviest items was the ammunition and gun; it was a cheap Belgian weapon I had bought at the ironmongers in Georgetown but it had exercised a fascination over the sergeant ever since I arrived; I had seen him playing with it, holding it to his shoulder and squinting down the barrel. Now he offered to buy it and the ammunition for twenty-five dollars, which was about what I had paid. I let him have it, and from then onwards never passed a day without seeing quantities of game.

Next day we set out again and reassembled at the place where I had left the stores, Yetto, Price, Sinclair, the horse, Maria, and myself, and began dividing up the loads and the duties. For his half-dollar a day a boy is assumed to be able to carry about fifty pounds for about twenty miles. It was Yetto's boast, of which the others were quick to take advantage, that he could carry a hundred pounds for fifty miles. I used to see them piling things on to Yetto's back and him taking them with pride and good humour. Relations were somewhat complicated by the fact that Price was not really under my orders at all. He was going on duty at Bon Success. He was new to the bush and did not like it. I made him groom and gave him the lamp and cooking utensils to carry. Sinclair was an odious youth anyway, but he knew a little about cooking. The other two hated him and on the last two days went without food altogether rather than take it from him. He asked if he might drive the ass and I said yes. He then made the point that it was impossible both to carry a pack and drive the ass who strayed all over the path and needed constant goading along. In point of fact Maria did nothing of the sort. She quickly got wise to the fact that if she stayed behind with the boys, they unslung their loads as soon as I was out of sight, and put them on her back. Accordingly she used to break away and trot along happily beside the horse. This was maddening for me, because every few miles her pack would work loose and she would start scattering bits of luggage along the trail and I would have to stop and rearrange things.

Every evening Yetto had complaints against Sinclair. 'Chief, dat boy no good at all. Him too young; him not know discipline.' Every day I used to decide to pay him off and send him back; then I used to think of Yetto's detestable cooking and hesitate. And on these occasions Sinclair always succeeded in putting me in a good temper. He would appear with my towel just when I wanted it; he would find a lime tree and unasked prepare me rum and lime when I returned from my bath in the creek; he knew exactly the things I should want, map, journal, fountain pen, glasses, and laid them out just where I needed them beside the hammock. So in spite of the fact that I knew him to be lazy, untruthful, disloyal, sulky and conceited, he remained in my service to the end as far as the frontier.

To this rather absurd little band there attached himself a spectral figure named Jagger. I had seen him, too, moping on the steps at Kurupukari and heard Mr Bain upbraiding him on more than one occasion on some obscure subject connected with the post office. He was a coloured youth in the technical Georgetown sense of the word and in that sense only; for I never saw a face so devoid of a nameable hue. It was a ghastly *grisaille* except for his eyes which were of a yellowish tinge, the colour of trodden snow, and circled with pink. He loped along with us carrying his own food and belongings, never asking for anything except company, always eager to help with advice. He spoke accurate and elaborate English, in a toneless, lisping voice that would have sounded supercilious had it not been accompanied by his expression of inflexible misery and self-disgust. He was ragged, destitute and extremely ill and was making for the Rupununi district as his last resource; going, he said, to visit friends, which was probably another way of saying that he was about to join that curious race of tramps who wander about the cattle country, there and in Brazil, living indefinitely on the open hospitality of the ranches.

His father had been a man of some substance. Jagger had been educated at a school and university in Scotland; he had married a Portuguese girl and cut rather a dash for some time in Georgetown. I never fully mastered the history of his downfall which was connected in some way with litigation, wills and moneylenders. Yetto explained it quite simply, 'Him was robbed by his brudders.'

He had fever badly, and on the second day arrived at the midday halt well behind the others, and dragging himself along unsteadily. He hung up his hammock, rolled into it and lay with averted face, unwilling to eat or talk. As I rode on that afternoon I began to worry about Jagger. It really looked as though he might be going to die on our hands; in his present state he would never reach the savannah on foot. Here I felt was the time for a Christian gentleman to show his principles; to emulate Sir Philip Sidney.

'Yetto,' I said that evening, 'I think that tomorrow Jagger had better ride my horse. I can easily walk the next few stages.'

'Dat's all right, chief,' said Yetto. 'Him not come on.'

'Not come on?'

'Him plenty sick. Him stay in his hammock, back where us had breakfast.'

'But will he be all right?'

'Oh yes, chief, him'll be all right. Him sick, dat's all.'

Later that evening half a dozen *vaqueiros* arrived with a drove of fifty cattle. I gave them quinine for Jagger and instructions to look after him, but I never heard whether or no he reached the savannah.

Various unsensational incidents stand out in my memory of this phase of the journey. A torrential rainstorm in which I arrived soaked through and through at the shelter two hours ahead of the outfit. I had been warned of the dangers in that climate of sitting about wet, so I stripped and made a fire. I must have looked an unseemly figure, stark naked except for hat and riding boots, scrabbling in the bush for dead wood. I had not made a fire since I was a Boy Scout fifteen years before. Contrary to all expectation it burned magnificently; I hung up my clothes round it on wooden props and they were soon steaming. Then I realized a thing that ought to have been obvious – that a fire needs constant refuelling. I went out again into the rain looking for wood, but without a cutlass could get very little. Then with very little compunction I tore up a large patch of the bark floor and substantial bits of the structure of the house and burned those. A week before I had been bitterly commenting on the Indians who had done the same, pointing out that it showed a peculiar trait in their racial character – a listlessness, improvidence, a wantonness, irresponsible egotism, arrested development – I had found numerous epithets to describe my contempt for their destructive habits.

A meeting on the trail with three Englishmen; one a rancher with a reputation for eccentricity; the other two naturalists who for some years had been tramping about tropical America in the pay of that last and now defunct survivor of the 'Fairy Godmother Departments', the Empire Marketing Board. The three were coming down together on foot. One had dysentery and looked deathly; the other two by contrast abnormally robust. They had just shot a 'bush turkey'. We stewed it and ate it together and then parted company, though not before one of the naturalists had caught a peculiar fly in the nostril of my horse.

A scare about a 'bad cow' which is what in England would be called a wild steer. This we learned about from the *vaqueiros* mentioned above to whose good attention I committed the wretched Jagger. The 'bad cow' had broken away from the drive and was last seen champing defiantly in the middle of the trail six or seven miles in front of us. There were deep creeks on either side of him which he was unlikely to cross alone, so that he would probably be in about the same place on the next day. He would charge at sight, the *vaqueiros* said. Accordingly I rode warily and with some misgiving when I got to the danger area. But it was all right. A tiger had got him the night before and the crows were already clustered round his carcass just where the *vaqueiros* said I would find him.

During the first week's ride, when I had been with Mr Bain, continually entertained by the fresh spate of his reminiscences, I had had practically no conversation with the boys. Now in the evenings, and particularly after wet days when I issued a ration of rum, I found them very sound company, particularly Yetto. I wish I could reproduce his manner of speech, but to attempt it would mean torturing the reader with phoneticisms. It was difficult to follow, being full of vowel sounds of immense breadth; the diction was Creolese with a curious admixture of rather unusual words such as 'weary', and 'matrimony'.

Like most people in the colony Yetto had done a variety of jobs in his time. He had formed one of the police guard of honour when the Prince of Wales visited Georgetown and the Prince had shaken hands with him. He had once set out on an ill-fated expedition to Cuba – a story which was introduced by: 'Chief, did you ever know a black man from Grenada named Adams?'

'No, I'm afraid not.'

'Him stole twenty dollars off of me.'

Adams had taken charge of the joint funds and absconded in Trinidad. Yetto had been married but had not liked it. He had seen the Georgetown riots. But the high summit of his experience had been a lucky strike as a 'pork knocker'. He had come back to Georgetown with 800 dollars and had spent it in six weeks.

'Why, Chief, me took an automobile and drove round and round de town with three girls and me give them gold bangles and went to all de best rum shops and hotels. But me didn't drink no rum, no chief, nor beer either. It was gin and whisky all de time. Me didn't get no sleep for days, driving round all night with the girls.'

'But tell me, Yetto, did you get any better girls for all this money you were spending?'

'No, Chief, just de same girls but me like to see dem happy. Dey was fine girls but you could get dem for a dollar a night. But me give dem gold bangles and gin and whisky and a drive round and round in an automobile. All de girls plenty fond of Yetto when he had de money . . . But me was young den. Now me learned wisdom.'

'What would you do if you had the money now?'

There was a pause and I expected Yetto to tell me that he would buy a farm or a shop and settle down from the arduous and unsettled life he was now living. 'Well, Chief, me tell you dis. Me would spend all de money on myself. Me would buy fine clothes and rings. Den de girls would go wid me for de hope of what me was going to give dem. And in de end me would give dem nothing.' And he opened his vast mouth and roared with laughter, his gold teeth flashing in the firelight.

But his pleasures had not been wholly philistine. During that rapturous six weeks an Italian opera singer had given a concert in Georgetown (. . . shadow and spangle of cheap tragedy . . . the ageing prima donna, Grand Dukes and English Milords behind her, pitifully touring like faint and ever widening ripples in a lake, in the company of her seedy and devoted manager, yearly to more remote and less lucrative audiences to the final, tartarean abyss of a Georgetown concert hall . . .)

'De cheapest ticket was two dollars but me went with my girl. Dere was all white people dere and de way her sung was wonderful, wid a different coloured dress for each song and dey was in all de languages, French and English and Italian and German and Spanish. Dat lady knew everything. Her made us cry.'

The last time that Yetto had come up the trail had been in the company of a government vet and his wife and the presence of the lady gave the occasion a peculiar lustre in Yetto's eyes. It had been altogether a very magnificent expedition with collapsible camp tables, picnic baskets and a cocktail shaker. They had travelled ten miles a day on foot with a troop of porters. Every place where they had halted was sanctified in Yetto's eyes. 'Dis is where Mrs McDougal shot an accouri.' . . . 'Dis is where Mrs McDougal was so weary dat Mr McDougal had to take off her boots.' . . . 'Dis is where Mrs McDougal had a bath.' . . . Yetto had not missed a detail of her habits or idiosyncrasies. 'Mrs McDougal had a great fancy for me. Her took my snapshot. Her said, "Now I must take Yetto," and her did. Doctor McDougal promised to send me a print. Tomorrow me show you de very tree where Mrs McDougal took my snapshot. When we get to Takama her say, "I don't know what we should have done without Yetto." Dere's nothing me wouldn't do for Mrs McDougal.'

On the third day from Kurupukari we crossed a dry creek and came into a little savannah named after the creek, Surana, where there was a large Indian village. These were sophisticated Macushis who were in constant contact with the ranches and the traffic of the trail. The men all wore shorts, grubby singlets and felt hats, the women cotton dresses. Some of them spoke a little English, some Portuguese; most of them had worked for Europeans at one time or another; there was a black man living among them, married to one of their girls. Altogether a highly cosmopolitan and contaminated lot, but even so, they had retained some of the characteristics of their race, particularly in the plan, or rather absence of plan, of the village.

'Large' must be interpreted in the local sense, in which a dozen huts make an important place, twenty something quite exceptional. Indeed I never saw a village as large as that though later in the Wapishiana country I slept at one where, I was told later, no less than twenty-two huts could be counted from one spot. But I arrived there after dark and set off at the first glimmer of dawn so that I never knew until later the size of the place.

About a dozen or fifteen huts could be seen at Surana. I believe there were others out of sight. The trail ran straight down the middle of the savannah, a bare streak. Half a dozen houses were built near it, but at considerable distances from one another. Tiny, meandering footpaths ran between them. Other huts lay half a mile or so away and, as always in Indian villages, there was a ruin or two and a house under construction. It was all very different from the compact, stockaded townships of Africa. A polite English-speaking young man came out to meet me and showed me an empty mud and thatched hut where I could spend the night, and the water hole, half a mile distant where I could wash. Later some of the women brought me a present of bananas. It was a hospitable place. Many of them assembled to stare and talk to the boys.

'Dey all love Yetto,' said Yetto.

That evening after supper Sinclair came to me leading an Indian and said, 'Chief, do you want to see this boy's arse?'

I misunderstood him and said no, somewhat sharply.

'Fine, young "arse",' said Sinclair. 'Your "arse" plenty weary. You want new "arse" to go Bon Success.' He further explained that Surana was so much beset by bats and tigers that the Indians left all their horses and cattle on the other side of the bush at Anai. The boy would come with us next day, and if I liked the look of his horse I could have it at a dollar a day for the rest of the journey. I should be needing two horses, because Maria had to go back to Kurupukari, so I closed with the offer.

Next day we reached Annai on the edge of the savannah. It was exhilarating to see open country again after the cramped weeks in the forest and the view from Annai at late evening was peculiarly fine; to the west lay the Pakaraima mountains; far away to the south the wooden tops of the Kanuku hills were just visible on the horizon; at our feet and before us lay the level savannah dotted with 'sandpaper' trees and broken in places by islands of bush; a high wind was blowing from the south.

Annai itself was simply a house, like the one at Kurupukari only slightly more dilapidated for no one lived there, the policeman in residence preferring a cosy outbuilding. There was glass in some of the windows for it had once been intended for a commissioner's residence but the boarding of the walls had warped and shrunk so that the wind whistled through the rooms, and I was obliged to put my pipe inside a boot before I could get it alight.

'Dat house is so healthy,' said Yetto, 'dat yo shiver all night.'

There were other occupants on the evening of my arrival; a surly Syrian, with a flabby white face, grotesque in riding clothes. He was a Georgetown business man who had lately acquired a share in the ranch of an aged Brazilian Negro and had been up to see to his interests; with him was a villainous-looking, wizened little Brazilian *vaqueiro*.

'Dat a very cruel man. Him tie up de Indians all night and beat dem until Mr Bain stop him.'

The Syrian asked me of the news in Georgetown and then said, 'What about the war?'

I supposed he meant the threatened breach between Colombia and Venezuela and I gave a vague description of the situation. 'No, no, I mean the war in Europe.'

'Unless it has broken out in the last fortnight there isn't one. Who did you think were fighting?'

'All of them You know, Germany and Italy and Russia and France and so on. That was what I heard. One of the boys got it from a *vaqueiro* who had heard it on the wireless at Boa Vista.' He sighed listlessly. 'Well, I'm glad there's nothing in it. Not that it affects me much.'

There was also a pleasant Spaniard named Orella and his wife coming down with a small drive of cattle. The wife was one of the daughters of Melville. They sent their love to the various relatives of theirs I should meet in the savannah, for, as I said earlier, almost everyone of importance in the Rapununi has some tie with the Melville family. The Spaniard and I dined together, leaving the Syrian and his *vaqueiro* to another table.

Yetto's predictions about the healthiness of the place proved quite accurate. It was deadly cold after the soft, close nights of the forest.

Next day was full of incident. I had arranged for horses the night before; a pack horse from the policeman and a riding horse from the Indian who had followed us from Surana. At dawn they went out to catch them but it was two hours before they brought them in. The policeman's horse was a stocky little grey, the Indian's a fiery chestnut stallion, larger than most of the local animals and six times more lifelike. He came in stepping high and tossing his head and was a difficulty from the first. He shied away from any attempt to saddle him until we made the discovery that he was blind on the off-side, having lately had his eye kicked in by a mare to whom his advances had been unwelcome. The bridle was altogether more difficult; he was not used to a bit and resisted by the simple expedient of rearing, striking out with his forefeet and throwing himself over on to his back. When he had done this twice, nearly braining the Indian and slewing his saddle rakishly under his belly, we gave up the idea of the bit and borrowed a Brazilian bridle with a barbed metal nose-piece. He took to that more kindly and at length, the saddle readjusted, fretted restlessly from foot to foot, his single eye rolling in a challenging fashion, ready to be mounted. Mr Orella who had been watching proceedings meditatively from the verandah gave it as his opinion that this was a fresh horse. However he allowed me to mount and as soon as I was in the saddle set off at a canter in the desired direction. After a mile he settled down to a brisk trot and I was able to enjoy the scenery and congratulate myself on at last having got a good ride.

The trail led along the foot of the hills, passed through them down a little valley and emerged again into the open grass land; there is usually a strong, blustering wind on the savannah. It was like being by the sea, to emerge into bright light and wide horizons after the twilit green tunnel through which we had come. I jogged along in the happiest frame of mind; if I had known how to, I should have sung. Suddenly after about ten miles the stallion stopped dead. I had no whip or spurs; I undid the leather hobble from his cheek strap and beat him; I kicked him as hard as I could. He stood four square and immovable. I thought something must be wrong with his harness, so dismounted and examined it; everything was in order. I tried to look at his feet but nothing would induce him to lift a hoof from the ground. I looked round for a stick but there was nothing in sight except sand and grass. I remounted and began the battle with heels and hobble. When I was practically exhausted he suddenly started off again and trotted another two miles. He was an odd horse. After two miles we reached a belt of bush; it was here, by a creek, that I had arranged to wait for the boys to catch up and cook breakfast. At the opening of the bush a thin log lay across the path. The stallion stopped again. The battle was resumed, but here I had the advantage for I was able to break off a stick. The stallion's answer was the one unfailing expedient. Quite slowly he stood up on his hind legs and performed the back somersault that he had been practising at Annai that morning. With an agility which I did not think it likely I could ever repeat, I managed to fall clear of him. He rolled for a little, shedding a stirrup leather; struck out with all four feet hopefully but inaccurately; then quietly got up, stepped over the log and began cropping the bush on the other side.

What with the fight and the fall I was fairly exhausted and felt thankful that this was our stopping place. I tethered him, unsaddled him, found the missing leather and decided that in the afternoon I would ride the grey and see how the boys could manage with a pack saddle on the stallion.

I was deadly thirsty and went down to the creek for water. It was perfectly dry except for one fetid puddle. I got a certain ignoble consolation from thinking that probably the horse was thirsty too. Then I lit a pipe and waited.

Yetto was the first to turn up and he immediately began on a story of Sinclair's misdoings that in my present rather dizzy state was quite unintelligible. Its conclusion, anyway, was that Yetto and Price had left Sinclair with the pack horse and that Sinclair did not know the way. Presently Price came loping in. He told me the story about Sinclair but it still made no sense. I sent him and Yetto up and downstream to see if there was a pool anywhere fit to drink. They came back after an hour without having found anything. At last Sinclair and the pack horse arrived. He began on his story but I had not the patience for it. I said I would hear it that night; meanwhile I was far too thirsty to eat anything; he was to saddle the pack horse and put the pack on the chestnut. I was going straight on.

It was a painful ride, the first of many that were to follow. The heat was intense, glaring up off the earth so that my face was skinned under the shade of a broad-brimmed hat. Exhaustion was infectious; I felt it seeping up from the stumbling horse, seeping down into him from me. Constant urging was necessary to keep him at a trot. When he fell into a walk the dead hardness of the saddle was intolerable. Above all there was thirst. Later I had many longer and hotter days without water, but this was the first of them and I was fresh from the deep shade and purling creeks of the forest. The trail, clear enough in places, would sometimes dwindle and peter out among patches of dried sedge; then it was necessary to cast round in widening circles until I picked it up again after a loss of time and strength. Often it would split and divide into two equally prominent branches. Then it was a matter of guessing to decide on the route; sometimes I went wrong and found the track I had been following led only to a dried water hole; then again it was necessary to cast for the real trail. In this way I must have covered nearly double the real distance, when at about five in the afternoon, I arrived at my destination.

This was the ranch of a man named Christie. I knew nothing about him except what I had been told the previous evening; that he was very old and 'very religious'. His religion, I was warned, took the form that he did not participate in the open hospitality of the savannah. He allowed – he could scarcely have prevented it – passers-by to hobble their horses in his corral and sleep under his shelter, but that was the full extent of his goodwill. Most people, riding through, if they could rely on their horses, made a double stage of it and got through to Annai in one day; others hung their hammocks in the open by the creek where I had left Yetto and the boys. However, there was no question of that for me; even if I had not had followers on foot, the horse could not have made any further effort; he was barely able to get so far. I had to risk the religious atmosphere and put up at Christie's.

Visibility is poor on the savannah by reason of the 'sandpaper' trees. These low shrubs, six or ten feet in height, are scattered loosely all over the country at intervals of twenty yards or so; sometimes they are thicker and from a distance give the impression of a copse, but when approached always resolve into isolated units; they throw almost no shade; their leaves are very rough on one side and it is from this peculiarity that they get their name; their wood is brittle and useless for any practical purpose. Their only good quality that I was able to discover was the element of surprise that they gave to travelling. In some countries one sees the day's objective from the start; it is there in front of one, hour after hour, mile after mile, just as remote, apparently, at noon as it had been at dawn; one's eyes dazzle with constant staring. The 'sandpaper' trees often hid a house from view – particularly the low, dun houses of the district – until one was practically inside it. Then there would be a sudden, exultant, a scarcely credulous, inward leap of delight as one realized, at the worst and almost desperate hour of the day, that one's distress was over. Horse and I were both unsteady with fatigue when an Indian home came into view quite near us. Then another, with some women squatting in front. They ran in and hid at my approach but I rode up to the door and shouted into the darkness, making the motions of drinking. After some giggling and nudging one of them brought me out a calabash of cold water. Then I said, 'Christie,' and they repeated, 'Christie', and giggled some more. Finally one of them came out and pointed in the direction I should take. Another twenty minutes brought me to the ranch. It was a handful of huts, thrown out haphazard on the ground like the waste stuff of a picnic party. There was no one about. I dismounted and walked round. The central and largest house was only half built but there was another near it with dilapidated thatch, open at all sides, which was distinguishable from the others by a plank floor, raised a couple of feet from the earth. Here, reclining in a hammock and sipping cold water from the spout of a white enamelled teapot, was Mr Christie.

He had a long white moustache and a white woolly head; his face was of the same sun-baked, fever-blanched colour as were most faces in the colony but of unmistakable Negro structure. It is illegal for blacks – or for that matter, whites, unless they get permission – to settle in Indian country and I learned that for the first ten years or so of his residence there had been repeated attempts by the Government to evict him; after that they had let him be. I greeted him and asked where I could water my horse. He smiled in a dreamy, absent-minded manner and said, 'I was expecting you. I was warned in a vision of your approach.'

He climbed out of the hammock, looked about for shoes, found only one, and hobbled across to shake hands with me.

'I always know the character of any visitors by the visions I have of them. Sometimes I see a pig or a jackal; often a ravaging tiger.'

I could not resist asking, 'And how did you see me?'

'As a sweetly toned harmonium,' said Mr Christie politely.

He pointed out the tenuous straggle of footpath that led to the water hole. I took off saddle and bridle and led the horse down by his rope halter. He whinnied at the smell of water and we both drank immoderately; he was trembling in the legs and lathered in sweat but, I was glad to find, not galled. I sluiced him down, turned him into the corral, and left him happily rolling in the dust. Then I slung my hammock under a shelter near Mr Christie's house and fell asleep until, two hours later, the rest of my party arrived. They had my change of clothes with them. As soon as they arrived I got out of boots and breeches, had a bath and a mug of rum. I drank a lot of rum that evening; how much I did not realize until next morning

63

when I discovered the empty bottle. Sinclair, knowing that there was a row in the air, had picked a handful of limes on his way. He filled up the mug assiduously with rum and limes and brown sugar and cold, rather muddy water. I did not investigate the boys' quarrel and Sinclair did not get the sack. The sweet and splendid spirit, the exhaustion of the day, its heat, thirst, hunger and the effects of the fall, the fantastic conversations of Mr Christie translated that evening and raised it a finger's breadth above reality.

The lamp stood on the floor in the middle of the shelter so that all the faces were illumined as faces are not meant to be seen; from below with cheek bones casting shadows across their eyes and strong light under the brows and chin and nostrils. Everyone in the vicinity came round to watch me eat supper. Mr Christie stalked round and round the lamp telling me about God.

He asked me whether I were a 'believer' and I said, yes, a Catholic.

'There are *some* good Catholics,' conceded Mr Christie, 'they are far from the truth but they are in the right direction. Only the other evening I was looking at the choir of the blessed singing before the throne of God and to my great surprise, I recognized the late Bishop of Guiana ... but they take too much on themselves. Their ministers like to be called "father". There is only one "Father" – the one above.'

'Have you the same objection to children addressing their male parent in that way?'

'It is a terrible thing to be a male parent' – Mr Christie had a large family by an Indian mistress – 'Verily it is written' – and he quoted some text I cannot remember to the effect that children are a curse. 'Why, only the other day my eldest son begat a child by a woman of no cultivation. He even speaks of marrying her.'

'But living as you do out here in the savannah, is lack of cultivation a very serious matter?'

'It is very serious when she will not sing,' said Mr Christie severely.

We spoke of the uncle of some friends of mine who had worked in this district as a missionary and retired to England as the result of a complete breakdown.

'That man had the devil in him,' said Mr Christie. 'Do you know what he did? He boiled a chicken in the place where I used to say my prayers. I have never been there since. It was defiled.'

I told him that the priest had since recovered his health and was working on the South Coast.

'No, no, I assure you that the contrary is the case. He appeared to me the other night and all the time he spoke to me his head rolled about the floor in a most horrible manner. So I knew he was still mad.'

Every Sunday he preached for four or five hours to the neighbouring Indians. I asked him whether his work among them was successful. 'No, not successful, you could not call it successful. I have been here for thirty years and so far have made no converts at all. Even my own family have the devil in them.'

He told me that he was at work on a translation of the scriptures into Macushi, 'but I have to change and omit a great deal. There is so much I do not agree with ... but I am not worried. I expect the end of the world shortly.' Some years back he had seen a number flashed in the sky and that was the number of days remaining. I asked him how he knew that that was the meaning of the number.

'What else could it be?' he asked.

As I sat soaking rum he told of numerous visions. How when his mistress died he had heard a voice from heaven say, 'The old horse is dead.'

'It did not mean that she was like a horse. In some ways she was very pretty. It meant no more riding for me.'

Lately he had been privileged to see the total assembly of the elect in heaven.

'Were there many of them?'

'It was hard to count because you see they had no bodies but my impression is that there were very few.'

I asked if he believed in the Trinity. 'Believe in it? I could not live without it. But the mistake the Catholics make is to call it a mystery. It is all quite simple to me.' He told me how the Pope had had a French admiral murdered and his heart sent to Rome in a gold box; also that Freemasons stole bodies out of the cemetery and kept them in a cellar below every Lodge. You could always tell a Freemason, he said, because they had VOL branded on their buttocks. 'It means volunteer, I suppose,' he said. 'I can't think why.'

Presently some of the onlookers in the outer circle came into the hut and squatted down round the lamp. I had some cocoa made and handed round. One of Mr Christie's daughters had married an East Indian. The man put a naked child on my knee and attempted to interest me in a row he was having with the policeman at Annai about illicit tobacco selling. It was all a trumped-up charge, he said, the result of spite. But I was not in the mood to follow his difficulties.

After a little I fell asleep and woke up to find the party still going on and Mr Christie still talking of visions and mystic numbers. When I next awoke they had all gone away, but I could hear Mr Christie prowling round in the darkness outside and muttering to himself.

FOUR

Daguar's ranch – Hart's ranch – St Ignatius Mission – Figuiredo – the
Boundary Commission

Next day was easy going. I started early and did the twenty-odd
miles to the next ranch before midday. The first half of the ride was
pleasantly cool, none of it was particularly disagreeable, for it is not
until afternoon, when the ground has got hot, that the savannah
becomes unendurable. When it is possible the *vaqueiros* stay under
cover and sleep from one until three. The horse was tired after the
bad time he had had the day before but he made the journey
successfully, with a little pushing in the last five miles, at the regular
four-mile-an-hour savannah trot.

The ranch I was making for was the property of a Georgetown
Chinaman named Mr Wong, who was one of Yetto's heroes on
account of his reputation for high play at cards. The manager, to
whom I had a note of introduction from Mr Bains, was a Portuguese
called d'Aguar or Da Guar or Daguar – opinion on the savannah
differed about the spelling. Anyway he was a swarthy, genial man,
with a well trained Indian mistress and a totally untrained little boy
of repulsive habits. The ranch was of very simple nature, three wattle
and mud huts in a wire enclosure, earth floored, thatch roofed, one
of them with a small verandah just long enough to sling a hammock,
but the enclosure was swept clean daily and there was a garden
beyond growing several sorts of vegetable. He was clever with his
fingers and the eaves of the hut were hung with bridles and whips
of plaited hide and ornamented saddles of his own making; most of
the ranchers are leather-workers during the wet season when the
plains are water-logged, and the damp in the air makes the raw hide
malleable. There was a certain swagger in Daguar's clothes, too; he
had a big-brimmed, leather-bound Brazilian hat, large silver buckles

67

down the sides of his leggings and a silver-hilted knife stuck into one of them; large spurs were strapped on to his bare, horny heels.

There were several pets, too; a grey monkey tied by his loins in the shade, a macaw and two or three green parrots on the rooftop, a gentle, perfectly tame deer, which he had caught as a baby and gelded. There were some cigarette cards nailed upon the supports of the house. The child, though naked, had an immense length of black hair coiled in a bun like an orthodox priest's, some artificial toys, made in Germany and bought in Georgetown. The Indian girl had a heliotrope dress of a material that glittered like wet seaweed, which she hastened to put on in our honour on my arrival. It was clearly a home on which was expended exceptional pride and care.

I asked the way to wash and was shown a path through the vegetable garden into a belt of bush. I went down and, pushing through, suddenly found a sharp precipice at my feet and a dark, swift river of some breadth. It was unexpected and dramatic after the great stretch of arid savannah all round. On the opposite side there was the same clay cliff and a fringe of bush; that was Brazil. I had not taken in – for the ranch was not marked on the map – that I was already at the frontier and that this was the Ireng. I was to see plenty of this river later on and grow to hate it. At the time I did not like it for the descent was slippery and coming up, clean from one's bath, one was covered with clay on hands and knees; also because I was bitten by countless small flies; also because I found the first tick on my body. Later I grew to think nothing of them, but I found this first one repulsive with his head deep and tenacious in my flesh, and his body swollen to the size of a pea. I burned him off and left the Ireng with some revulsion.

The bites itched all the afternoon. Daguar explained that the cabouri fly was troublesome in this district even in dry weather. In the rains it was impossible to go out of doors without gloves and a towel muffled round the head. They are odious little insects, so small that they easily penetrate any ordinary mosquito curtain; they breed in running water and attack in great numbers. Several books about the neighbourhood describe them as completely covering every exposed surface of the writer, so that no skin was visible at all. You cannot feel their bite until they have finished sucking; then they leave a little black spot behind them and a circle of burning flesh. But they are less formidable than the mosquito because, so far as is known, they do not carry fever, they will not bite through even the thinnest clothes, they are instantly dispersed by winds or darkness.

Insects played a fairly prominent part in my experience throughout all this period. For the preceding week I had been discomforted by *bêtes rouges*, a minute red creature which brushes off the leaves of the bush on to one's clothes and finds its way below one's skin where it causes unendurable itching. My arms and legs were covered with these in spite of crab oil and antiseptic soap and I scratched until I was raw. I cured them temporarily at St Ignatius but picked them up again as soon as I was on the move. It is quite accurate to say that in the weeks from leaving Kurupukari until some time after my final return to Georgetown, there was not a two-inch square on my body that was not itching at some time of the day or night.

When the boys arrived I told Yetto to cook breakfast† but he said that Mrs Daguar was getting me some. Presently she brought it, a dish of fried eggs, minced *tasso* fried with herbs, bananas and delicious Brazilian coffee; she had china and cups and glasses and knives and forks and even a tablecloth. I asked her how she became such an excellent cook and she said she had worked for one of the Melvilles before she took up with Daguar. I had with me a number of Woolworth necklaces and bracelets which I had bought in London for barter and was in some doubt whether this woman was too grand to like them. However, I tried one on the child and the mother was so evidently delighted that I gave another to her with complete success. That and a glass of rum to Daguar put us all on a very friendly basis and he volunteered to lend me another horse to take me to Mr Hart's, the ranch where I was bound next day.

A Portuguese family came to call that afternoon with a guitar which they played. They all came in and solemnly shook hands with me – about eight of them – on arrival and on departure. (I suppose English people abroad must be constantly giving offence by not shaking hands often enough. It never occurs to us. I once travelled in a French ship where every passenger shook every other passenger's hand every morning.)

Two wild-eyed, shaggy Patamona Indians also arrived in a canoe from upstream, trying to trade a monkey for some gunpowder, for

† Luncheon was always called breakfast in this country.

Wong's ranch is at one extreme angle of the savannah, the nearest civilized spot to the Pakaraima district.

The boys spent the afternoon washing clothes and drying them in the sun. Yetto was still as cheerful as ever but Price had got noticeably thinner since I first met him at Takama. He did not like his rations and he did not like walking and he did not like Sinclair. I think it was this last trouble that upset him more than anything. Half the bad feeling was because Sinclair took for himself and never shared out whatever was left over from my meals – and I noticed that he always prepared twice as much as I needed. But there were only two more days to Bon Success where I should be leaving all three of them and I did not propose to involve myself in their squabble.

Next day a fresh horse and an early start brought me to Pirara by eleven in the morning. On the map a large lake is marked, called Amuku. I was surprised not to see this but learned that it had never existed. Schomburgh, the explorer, had camped there in the last century and found a patch of land temporarily inundated; the cartographers have recopied it from one another ever since.

The village of Pirara, on the other hand – another prominent feature of the map – did once exist, not indeed in recent memory but in reliable records. Now both Amuku and Pirara are bare savannah and the name Pirara is used of the ranch about five miles to the east of the place marked on the map, owned by Mr Hart, an American married to another of the Melville daughters. It is one of the most imposing and important houses in the district, *the* most important next to Dadanawa. Its unique and most famous feature is a wind wheel which draws water and works a variety of machines in the workshop. This is a landmark all over the plain, though to my inexperienced eye it was indistinguishable from a palm tree except at the shortest range. It seriously worried me in fact, because Daguar had told me that I should see it from, at the very least, ten miles off and, not seeing it, I began to think that I was on the wrong trail, and fretted increasingly until at length, of the countless tall trees with circular summits one seemed outstandingly rigid and symmetrical and gradual approach revealed it as Mr Hart's wind wheel.

Mr Hart was still away – it was his disastrous drive whose carcasses we had encountered all the way up the trail – but Mrs Hart received me with the utmost kindness. She had a tumultuous family of sons under the precarious control of an attractive Creole governess in shorts; lithe and vital as an adolescent Josephine Baker. Their school hours seemed mostly spent in reciting the rosary and getting whipped.

The house, like all tropical houses, was a collection of separate buildings; the main one was shingle-built, with floors, doors and even ceilings; I was given the schoolroom for my hammock; there were framed pictures on the walls, looking-glasses and several shelves of books. Across the yard was a shower bath. There were large fruit trees all round – mangoes, soursap, grapefruit, lemon and orange, breadfruit and custard apple; there was a flower garden with pebble paths; there was fresh pork for breakfast; most sensational of all there was a motor truck standing outside, as unexpected and incongruous an object as it would have been in the Piazza at Venice. It was the only mechanical vehicle between Georgetown and Manaos. It had belonged, I was told, to a German who had once been taken with the idea that crops up fruitlessly from time to time of improving Boa Vista. After his rout Mr Hart bought it and with infinite difficulty got it to Pirara. He could seldom afford to use it himself on account of the enormous price of benzine in the neighbourhood and indeed there were few directions in which it could have been driven. At the moment, however, it was doing service for the Government in carrying Boundary Commission stores from their dump at Yupukarri to Bon Success.

I heard a good deal about this Boundary Commission and later came into contact with part of it. Like all activities of Government it was, no doubt unjustly, one of the jokes of the colony. It is notorious that South American states are in frequent conflict about inaccessible bits of territory. At the beginning of this century Brazil claimed the whole of the Rupununi savannah, while there was very nearly war between Great Britain and Venezuela over the north-west frontier. Arbitrators were able to avert hostilities in both cases, but the boundaries as defined by them remained vague, as they were plotted on blank or conjectural maps in reference to hills or rivers that had never been surveyed and whose existence in some cases was only assumed from Indian report. A joint commission of the states involved had accordingly gone out to survey and demarcate the frontiers, to find which of the numerous confluent streams of the Takutu and Courantyne were in fact the rivers and which the tributaries, whether the brown patches marked on all the maps as Akarai mountains corresponded to any real geographical feature, and other disputed points that could only be decided by first-hand investigation. The Brazilians had been led to expect a detachment of Royal Engineers and suffered some disappointment and resentment, it was freely said in the colony, when, the two parties having painfully converged and established contact, they discovered a number of local surveyors racially representative of the mixed population of Georgetown. The Commission had been at work for some time, but had so far only surveyed the single section of the line that was already accurately known; their main achievement to date was the division of Mount Roraima, where the British, Brazilian and Venezuelan boundaries meet, so that the colony was left with only a precipitous face of bare rock, and the brass plate erected by Lady Clementi to commemorate her visit there became foreign property. Their activities, however, had necessitated a good deal of moving of stores and consequent recruiting of labour from villages hitherto untouched by civilization, with the result that wages in the form of celluloid combs, printed cottons, and even gramophones were to be found in unlikely places. There was also the secondary effect, much complained of by the ranchers, that labour was scarce, for the Indians only come out to work when they need some specific object, usually a gun or ammunition, and could subsist happily on the glut of government stores for months to come.

As I have mentioned there were books at Pirara – a curious library, much ravaged by ants, filled, like the boxes outside secondhand booksellers, with works on every conceivable subject, hygiene, carpentry, religion, philosophy, and among them a number of fairly recent best-sellers left presumably from time to time by passing travellers. As I was looking through them I came upon a local mission magazine in which were extracts from the diaries of Father Carey-Elwes, the priest who had first penetrated into the Indian village of the border and hill country. Two days dealt with the writer's first acquaintance with Mr Christie many years before, and I was enchanted to discover a description corresponding almost exactly to my own experience; enchanted and somewhat relieved,

72

for in the last two days I had begun to doubt whether the whole of that fantastic evening had not been an illusion born of rum and exhaustion. One anecdote seemed to me so delightful that I cannot forbear to repeat it. At the end of his stay Father Carey-Elwes offered his host one of the medals of Our Lady which he carried for distribution among his converts. The old man studied it for a moment and returned it saying (I quote from memory), 'Why should I require an image of someone I see so frequently? Besides, it is an exceedingly poor likeness.'

Next day's journey lay through Bon Success where Mr Teddy Melville lived; he is one of Mrs Hart's brothers and holds the government rank of Ranger. She had not seen him for some time and accordingly kindly offered to drive me there in the motor van. Sinclair and Price were by now visibly exhausted by their unwonted exercise and, comparatively easy as my own journey had been, I too had grown tired in the successive wearying days on horseback, the continuous saddling and bridling, watering and grooming, the early start to avoid the heat of the day, the stiff and sticky wait until the rest of the party arrived with soap and change of clothes – so I gratefully accepted her offer.

Daguar's horse and the stallion – somewhat sobered by now – were to be called for by Yetto and Sinclair on their return journey. There is a casualness in the ranchers' treatment of horses, other than their own favourite mounts, that at first seemed surprising after the exaggerated importance with which they are treated in England. Very few people on the savannah could tell you exactly how many horses they possessed or where they were. At the annual round-ups they are identified by their brands, sorted out and taken home. For the rest of the time they wander at pasture, often straying twenty or thirty miles. Borrowed horses are left about and fetched when needed like books in England. Of course a horse in that country is worth about a tenth of its price in England. One can buy a reasonably strong eight-year-old pony for five pounds or less.

We did the twenty miles or so to Bon Success in a third of the time it would have taken by horse but during that time the going was incomparably rougher. Mrs Hart, a son, the driver and myself sat on the wooden seat in front; the boys lay with the luggage behind and we were all thrown up and down and from side to side as the car jolted over the grass beside the trail. Ground that seemed smooth enough on foot was scarcely passable on wheels. I soon realized why no one else thought it worth while investing in a car. There were two considerable creeks to get through. We had to cut dried wood and lay a way across them, then haul the car up the opposite bank with chain and pulleys. But we got to Bon Success well before noon and breakfasted with Teddy Melville and his enchanting little Brazilian wife. We slept for an hour and then drove on up the course of the Takutu another two miles to St Ignatius, where I was to spend ten days as the guest of Father Mather, the kindest and most generous of all the hosts of the colony.

He was at work in his carpenter's shop when we arrived and came out to greet us, dusting the shavings off his khaki shirt and trousers, and presenting a complete antithesis of the 'wily Jesuit' of popular tradition. Like all his Society, Father Mather is a self-effacing man and I think he would not relish any further personal description. He is a skilled and conscientious craftsman; everything he does, from developing films to making saddles, is done with patient accuracy. Most of the simple furniture of the living-room was his work – firm, finely jointed and fitted, delicately finished, a marked contrast to the botched, makeshift stuff that prevailed even in Georgetown. He loves and studies all natural things, in particular woods and birds about which he has huge stores of first-hand knowledge. It is very rarely that he goes down to the coast; when he does the river-side scenery – to me unendurably monotonous – provides a luxurious orgy of observation; occasionally some call will take him into the hills, but for the most part his work keeps him in the desolate surroundings of St Ignatius, and his researches are confined to the insects that collect round his reading-lamp in the evenings.

I paid off Yetto, Sinclair and Price and they went away, Price to the station at Bon Success, Yetto and Sinclair back down the trail, for blacks are not encouraged to stay long among the Indians. Before they left they each asked to be photographed and in turn wore Yetto's old cloth cap and Price's spotted handkerchief for their portraits. Mrs Hart had tea, chatted for an hour and drove off. The first phase of the journey was over.

All the time I was in Guiana I found myself remarking on the contrast it offered to Africa. St Ignatius was very unlike the missions

74

I had seen there – the crowded compounds, big school houses with their rows of woolly black heads patiently absorbing 'education'; the solid presbyteries and packed, devout congregations; the native priests and nuns, methodical in white linen and topees; the troops of black children veiled for their first Communion; the plain chant and the examination papers. It was as lonely an outpost of religion as you could find anywhere. If it had not been for the Calvary on the river-bank, it might have been one of the smaller ranches. It was, in fact, a ranch also, for without cattle no one can live on the savannah; and the head *vaqueiro* was later to prove of the greatest service to me. Like all the savannah houses it was invisible from quite a short distance. The main building was made of wattle mud, thatch, timber and corrugated iron; a home far smaller and less imposing than Pirara or Annai, but, unlike them, distinguished by a second storey with a gallery of loose planks running the length of it. The walls of the upper rooms came short of the eaves and the high savannah wind swept and eddied through them, while the timbers swayed and creaked and the thatch and iron above seemed to heave and belly, so that at night one felt as though one were at sea in a sailing ship. Downstairs there was a single small living-room, a kitchen, and store-rooms; above there were not only bedrooms but, in one of them, an iron bedstead, mattresses, and pillow, where I was put to sleep. This, a bright reading lamp, bread and pure English conversation were luxuries I found here which I had greatly missed on the journey up.

Near the house was a small church built of tin and thatch and furnished with a few benches six inches high from the mud floor; it was open at the west end for light and ventilation, and in spite of every discouragement and a barrier of wire netting, a hen used regularly to lay her eggs behind the altar. Some way from the church stood Father Mather's workshop where every kind of odd job in leather, iron and wood was brilliantly performed. Further away still was a little shelter used as a school house for a dozen or so Indian children who appeared irregularly to learn from a kindly Indian teacher. There were several Indian houses scattered within a mile's radius of the mission who kept a close liaison with it. There was a wired corral and a *vaqueiros*' hut. There was a large, slightly dilapidated barn where visiting Indians put up.

Here Father Mather lived quite alone for the greater part of the year. Another priest, Father Keary, used the home as his headquarters, but except in the wet weather he was continually on circuit among the villages. Father Mather kept the home going and managed the ranch and stores; he attended to the Indians in the immediate vicinity and dispensed medicines and first aid. Most of the ranchers on the British side and all the Brazilians were Catholics and he saw to their needs, baptizing and marrying and burying them. He repaired the boats and harness and the fabric of the house. He had once been desperately ill from fever and had frequent slighter recurrences; he had constant toothache for he was two hundred miles from the nearest dentist; he was one of the happiest men I met in the country.

I have often observed that the servants of the religious are, as a class, of abnormally low mentality. I do not know why this should be – whether it is that good people in their charity give jobs to those whom no one else will employ, or whether, being poor, they get them cheap, or whether they welcome inefficient service as a mortification, or whether unremitting association with people of superior virtue eventually drives sane servants off their heads. Whatever the explanation, that is usually the state of affairs. Father Mather's establishment, however, was an exception. It is true that there was an idiot Macushi boy who constantly obtruded a moon face round the door at meal times, asking for tobacco, but he was employed only on casual labour outside the house. The two Indian widows who cooked, wove hammocks, drove the guinea fowl out of the bedrooms and generally 'did for us' were exemplary people. So was David Max y Hung, the head *vaqueiro* mentioned above. This pious and efficient young man spoke two Indian languages, English and Portuguese perfectly. He was half Chinese, half Arawak Indian and his wife was Brazilian. He was away at a round-up at the time of my arrival (every ranch sends a representative to every round-up to identify his own cattle and see that there is no tampering with the brands) and it was his absence that prolonged my stay so pleasantly, for on the first evening Father Mather explained to me that it was quite hopeless to think of reaching Boa Vista by canoe at that season. It was easy, however, to ride there, and on David's return I could have horses and David himself for a guide. So I stayed on, glad of the rest and learning hourly from Father Mather more about the country, for a week until David returned, and a final three days while horses were being got in and baggage repacked.

They were peaceful and delight days. Mass at seven in the little church where sometimes half a dozen Indians would appear, always the school teacher and the idiot boy; then coffee; then Father Mather would go off to his workshop and I would sit and read in a long chair in the windswept gallery or make tracings from maps at the table downstairs. There were a quantity of maps of varying value, mostly roughly sketched plans of journeys in the hills and round the savannah, and gradually I was able to correct my official map until it had some semblance of accuracy. Breakfast at noon and then Father Mather returned to his business. At sundown we used to go down to the river to wash (one does not do much swimming in these rivers because they are full of dangerous creatures – sting ray, electric eels and carnivorous fish); supper at seven, and after supper we smoked and talked until bedtime about Guiana or England while Father Mather sorted out photographs or insects or feathers. During these evenings I learned to cut up, consume and eventually even to enjoy the pungent black tobacco of the district.

There were pets, of course; a misanthropic and rather menacing 'bush turkey' which strutted about the gallery, shaking his scarlet dewlap; two toucans with vast, disproportionate beaks, shaped and coloured like toys; they used to appear at meal times and catch pieces of bread with astonishing accuracy; if neglected they asserted their presence by pecking one sharply in the leg. There was a mischievous little mocking-bird who upset everything and to whom I became particularly attached; he was killed by a cat during my stay. There was also a huge toad who inhabited the house, though he can scarcely be described as a pet; he had quarters behind a kerosene tin and woke up at sunset with a series of deep barks; he never appeared except by lamplight when he would come out, flopping along heavily; he had an unaccountable taste for burning cigarette ends which he would snap up and swallow with an insatiable appetite.†

There were a few callers because the mission lay on the cattle trail

† I mentioned this phenomenon later to Mr Winter, who told me he had once seen a toad eat a burning cigar end outside an hotel in Georgetown but that no one would ever believe him.

at Dadanawa and it is uncivil in that district to pass any house without stopping to greet the inhabitants. The manager of the company's ranch came to coffee one morning. He was riding a fine, corn-fed horse, and habitually did the journey from Bon Success to Dadanawa in one day. On another occasion Mr Gore, the next neighbour up the trail passed us with a drove of cattle and stopped for supper. He had had a wandering life and told stories of the Yukon gold rush, but he had now married an Indian and settled in the Rupununi for good. Teddy Melville came by with an ostentatiously armed policeman, on his way to investigate a story of 'pork knockers' in Indian territory beyond Wichabai. And besides more formal visitors there were usually a dozen or so nondescript strangers hanging about the house. Some were Brazilians, in or out of jobs, or calling on relatives at ranches this side of the border; others were Indians come to trade, bringing in pelts, honey, *farine*, game or fish to exchange for cloth or shot. There was never any bargaining with these traders. They took what they were offered with completely impassive faces. Usually Father Mather led them into the store and let them see what he had. They could go on choosing until they had made up the value of what they had brought. Occasionally they would have taken all that attracted them before they had exhausted their credit. Then they would make as though to go and he would force some further object on them. They would take it listlessly like everything else, and drift away to their homes. Sometimes there were Indians with injuries or illnesses asking for medical attention. Sometimes they had no apparent motive in their visit but had come for a few days' gossip, or were halting on a journey, moved invisibly like the tides, on some unexplained, pointless errand.

The life of the Brazilian frontier must, I should think, be unique in the British Empire. In its whole length from Mount Roraima to the Courantyne – a distance of about five hundred miles – Bon Success is the only British government station, and that is under the admirable management of Mr Melville, who is half Indian by birth and married to a Brazilian. On the other side there is no representative of law nearer than Boa Vista. There is no comic 'Beachcomber' administrator dressing at night for dinner and whistling his old school song as the colours are lowered at sunset; there are no flags, no military, no customs, no passport examinations, no immigration forms. The Indians have probably very little idea of whether they are on British or Brazilian territory; they wander to and fro across the border exactly as they did before the days of Raleigh.

Throughout the whole district, too, there is only one shop and that is in two parts, half in Brazil and half in British Guiana. The proprietor is a Portuguese named Mr Figuiredo. He lives immediately opposite Mr Melville and he takes good care to keep his dealings strictly legal. On his own side of the river he sells things of Brazilian origin, hardware, ammunition, alcohol in various unpalatable forms, sugar and *farine*, a few decayed-looking tins of fruit and sweets, tobacco, horses, saddlery and second-hand odds and ends extorted from bankrupt ranchers; on the British side he sells things brought up from Georgetown, mostly male and female clothing, soaps and hair oils, for which the more sophisticated Indians have a quite unsophisticated relish, and brands of patent medicines with engraved, pictorial labels and unfamiliar names – 'Radways Rapid Relief', 'Canadian Healing Oil', 'Lydia Pynkham's Vegetable Product'. If a Brazilian wants anything from the British side he and Mr Figuiredo paddle across the river and he buys it there; and vice versa. Any guilt of smuggling attaches to the customer.

Father Mather and I went to breakfast with Mr Figuiredo one day. He gave us course after course of food – stewed *tasso* with rice, minced *tasso* with *farine*, fresh beef with sweet potatoes, fresh pork, fried eggs, bananas, tinned peaches and *crème de Cacao* of local distillation. His women folk were made to stand outside while we ate, with the exception of one handsome daughter who waited. After breakfast we went into the shop and Mr Figuiredo made an effortless and unembarrassing transition from host to shopkeeper, climbing behind the counter and arguing genially about the price of coffee. He has no competition within two hundred miles and his prices are enormous; many ranchers pay their wage bill in chits at his store; even allowing for the expense and risk of transport his profits must be exceptional, but he lives in a very simple fashion, dressing always in an old suit of pyjamas and employing his family to do the work of the house. His ambition is to save enough to leave Brazil altogether and retire to Portugal.

Once or twice Father Mather and I paid visits to neighbouring Indians, but even these comparatively civilized people were very elusive; at one little group of houses all the men were away on a hunting expedition; at another the whole population had migrated to their cassava fields in the hills. Those we met were intensely shy except for one elderly women who was reputed to be a 'piai woman'.† She had an old felt hat, long straggling hair and a filthy calico dress; her upper lip was tattooed with a blue moustache. She was extremely friendly, kissed our hands and gave us a calabash of home-brewed liquor.

After a week David returned from the round-up – suave, spectacled, faultlessly efficient – and took over the arrangements for my journey to Boa Vista. The ranches on the other side lay along the banks of the Takutu and the Rio Branco; this, though circuitous, was the normal route which could be done in five or six days. It was possible, however, to travel direct across the savannah in three days and, to David's unexpressed regret, I decided to do this. My luggage was now reduced to a rucksack and a canvas grip, so that its transport presented no serious difficulty. I was assured of ample provisions at Boa Vista and for the short crossing would take the luck of the country. Father Mather added bread and chocolate. On the morning of our departure he made me two presents, typical of him and of the country. I had casually mentioned, early in my stay, that I wished I had brought with me some kind of case for my camera. Later I noticed him measuring it but did not know the reason until he appeared with a perfectly fitting case, covered with deer skin and lined with flannel, on a foundation of galvanized iron; there was even a waterproof envelope for it kept in place by a band cut from an old bicycle tyre. He also gave me two pieces of rare local wood shaped up for conversion into walking sticks, gummed over and wrapped in waterproof paper to protect them from damage.

David's Brazilian brother-in-law Francisco joined us; the luggage was divided – unequally, for I took only hammock, blanket and change of clothes – between our three horses. Then after breakfast on February 1st, we set off for the border. The sun was obscured and a light drizzle of rain was falling.

† Witch.

FIVE

The ford was about three miles upstream from St Ignatius. As I
have said, there were no formalities of any sort in crossing the
boundary; our horses waded through the shallow water, stretching
forward to drink; half-way over we were in Brazil. A lurch and
scramble up the opposite bank; we forced our way through the fringe
of bush, leaning low in the saddle to guard our faces from the thorn
branches; then we were out into open country again, flat and
desolate as the savannah we had left; more desolate, for here there
was no vestige of life; no cattle track, no stray animals; simply the
empty plain; sparse, colourless grass; ant-hills; 'sandpaper' trees; an
occasional clump of ragged palm; grey sky, gusts of wind, and a dull
sweep of rain.

We rode on until sunset, Francisco in front showing the way, then
myself; at the back David who had chosen the worst horse. I never
saw anyone take so much trouble with his horse as Francisco. Every
few miles he would dismount, slacken the girths and peer under his
saddle for signs of galling. Brazilian saddles are built on a wooden
frame, padded with straw like the packing of wine bottles. He had
a ragged blanket below the straw which he would repeatedly shake
out and refold. I got impatient at these frequent stops but Francisco
proved right in the end for he was the only one of us who got his
horse to Boa Vista with a whole back.

At sunset the horses raised their heads and quickened their pace.
It was intensely dark and we could only follow by the creaking of
the harness ahead. At length we came to a stop and a blacker
darkness in front proved to be a *vaqueiros*' out-station. Francisco and

David called out in Portuguese and were presently answered by a man's voice. Some minutes later very small light appeared in the hands of a small boy. It revealed a typical thatched shelter with mud floor and breast-high mud walls, of the sort to which I had by now grown accustomed; also an elderly man who came out to shake our hands. In the shadows were half a dozen hammocks whose occupants peered at us and rolled over again to sleep. A second light glowed dimly beyond, in a room where the women had been roused to make us some supper. Francisco and David led off the horses to water at a nearby creek; the small boy dragged out a box for me to sit on; finding I could not speak Portuguese the elderly man contented himself by sitting astride his hammock and staring at me gloomily. After about ten minutes the boy brought me a minute cup of black coffee, thick and sweet, as coffee is always made in the countries that grow and understand it. There was a table at one side of the room, built on piles driven into the floor; when David and Francisco returned the man motioned us to draw up our boxes and sit there; the lamp stood in the centre. It consisted of a little bowl of beef fat with a couple of inches of wick hanging over the edge and giving a smoky, orange flame. A woman brought in a tin pot of stewed *tasso* and another of *farine*. We had our own plates, knives and forks. David and Francisco helped themselves liberally. I attempted, in politeness, to eat a little but found it impossible to swallow. David, with an explanation to our host of this curious English taste, produced the bread. I soaked a slice in the tasteless, greasy water of the stew and ate it. Later when the others were in their hammocks I supplemented this meagre dinner with some of Father Mather's chocolate.

The thatch above our heads was very old and partially rotten. Even in the flickering light of the dip we could see moving across it the shadows of lizards and huge spiders; presumably it was also full of scorpions. Its reek was overpowering – a mixture of wet spaniel and turnip fields, so pungent that for hours I could not sleep and even contemplated taking my hammock outside and looking for other shelter under the trees. Eventually, however, I lost consciousness and was awakened at grey dawn by David to say that the horses were saddled and that we had a long day in front of us.

It proved to be by far the hardest day I had yet done. The rain had passed over and the sun came up, blinding and burning; there was no wind. With two brief halts we rode steadily until half an hour before sunset. Two hours after our start we stopped at an Indian house to make tea and eat some dry bread. After that, until evening, we got no water. The stream where we stopped at noon was dry except for a few thick puddles, good enough for washing down the horses but not fit for drinking. Without water, I found, one lost all appetite for food, and I left the stale bread and tinned sausage untouched in my pocket.† All through the blazing afternoon I found that I thought of nothing except drinking. I told myself very simple stories which consisted of my walking to the bar of my club and ordering one after another frosted glasses of orange juice; I imagined myself at a plage, sipping ice-cold lemon squashes under a striped umbrella, beside translucent blue water. I constructed 'still lives' of bottles and syphons, glass goblets of bitter Hereford cider, jugs of peaches soaking in hock and champagne, even effervescing tumblers of liver salts. It was interesting that the drinks I thought of were nearly all fruity – no foaming tankards of ale or cellar-cool wine.

At last that day, like all others, came to an end. When I was unsteady in the saddle with exhaustion and the sun lay low and straight in our eyes, we came to a flowing creek and a hut beyond it. The horses could not be got past the water, nor had we any inclination to urge them. We drank mug after mug of the cold stream and then, very stiffly, climbed up the bank to greet our host, a curly-headed half-caste. As he was bringing out the inevitable *farine* and *tasso*, I slung my hammock; sat down in it to wait; lay down, and awoke in my clothes eleven hours later to find dawn breaking and the horses already saddled.

The next two days were easy going and uneventful except for our passing a black jaguar and an ant bear. The jaguar was a mere shadow, slipping away from us in the distance; I did not learn until later that it was a beast of some rarity. The ant bear, though common enough, was vastly more impressive, like something from an earlier phase of creation; the size and colour of an Irish wolf-hound with an absurdly attenuated nose, and a tail as long as itself, curled and

† For some reason no one travels with water in this country; chiefly I suppose because every ounce of weight is considerable, and also because at most times in the year the place is well watered. Anyway the pint or so of tepid liquid which one could have taken in a flask would have been negligible against the thirst of twelve hours in the sun.

feathery; it loped along lethargically within a few yards of us, either oblivious or indifferent to our approach.

We had now reached the inhabited Rio Branco district and we slept at a large ranch house, distinguished by a primitive sugar mill, round which an ox plodded to the constant shouting of an Indian boy. A rich smell of toffee arose from the copper cauldrons. The process resulted in stone-hard cakes of candy, one of which was presented to each of us on leaving and happily gnawed up by David and Francisco. The proprietor dispensed patriarchal hospitality to twenty or more strangers and workmen. We dined in three shifts, the company waiting patiently on benches to take the first vacant place at the table; they were of all races and ranks, including a one-eyed Negro, a deaf and dumb Indian, and an elegant young man in imitation silk pyjamas who hiccoughed extravagantly. The fare was the usual *farine* and *tasso*, enriched with milk and treacle. David did all the conversation necessary at these visits, performing greetings and introductions and expressing our thanks with infinite courtesy and giving an impression of such distinction that, here, we were allowed to sling our hammocks in the verandah of the house instead of in the crowded shed outside. On the fourth day we reached the bank of the Rio Branco at an empty hut immediately opposite Boa Vista.

Since the evening at Kurupukari when Mr Bain had first mentioned its name, Boa Vista had come to assume greater and greater importance to me. Father Mather had only been there once, and then in the worst stage of malignant malaria, so that he had been able to tell me little about it except that some German nuns had proved deft and devoted nurses. Everybody else, however, and particularly David, had spoken of it as a town of dazzling attraction. Whatever I had looked for in vain at Figuiredo's store was, he told me, procurable at 'Boa Vist''; Mr Daguar had extolled its modernity and luxury – electric light, cafés, fine buildings, women, politics, murders. Mr Bain had told of the fast motor launches, plying constantly between there and Manaos. I had come to regard it as Middle Western Americans look on Paris, as Chekhov peasants on St Petersburg. In the discomfort of the journey there, I had looked forward to the soft living of Boa Vista, feeling that these asperities were, in fact, a suitable contrast, preparing my senses for a fuller

84

appreciation of the good things in store. So confident was I that when we first came in sight of the ramshackle huddle of buildings on the further bank, I was quite uncritical and conscious of no emotion except delight and expectation.

The river was enormously broad and very low; so low that as we gazed at the town across sand dunes and channels and a fair-sized island it seemed to be perched on a citadel, instead of being, as was actually the case, at the same dead level as the rest of the plain. Two *vaqueiros* were lying in hammocks by the bank, and from these David elicited the information that a boat was expected some time in the next few hours to ferry them across. There was a corral by the hut into which we turned the horses; then we carried the saddles and baggage down the precipitous path to the water's edge and settled ourselves to wait. The *vaqueiros* studied us with an air that I came to recognize as characteristic of Boa Vista; it was utterly unlike the open geniality of the ranches, conveying, as it did, in equal degrees, contempt, suspicion and the suggestion that only listlessness preserved us from active insult.

With David's assistance, I began some inquiries about accommodation. There was none, they said.

'But I understood there were two excellent hotels.'

'Ah, that was in the days of the Company. There was all kinds of foolishness in the days of the Company. There is nowhere now. There has not been an hotel for two years.'

'Then where do strangers stay?'

'Strangers do not come to Boa Vist'. If they come on business, the people they have business with put them up.'

I explained that I was on the way to Manaos and had to wait for a boat. They showed complete indifference, only remarking that they did not know of any boat to Manaos. Then one of them added that possibly the foreign priests would do something for me – unless they had left; last time he was in Boa Vist' the foreign priests were all sick; most people were sick in Boa Vist'. Then the two men started talking to each other, with the obvious desire of terminating our conversation.

My enthusiasm had already cooled considerably by the time we saw a boat put out from the opposite shore and make slowly towards us. The owner of the boat had business at the ranch on our side and made no difficulty about lending it. We all got in, his boy, David,

Francisco, I, the two surly *vaqueiros*, the saddles and the baggage, so that the gunwales were only an inch clear of the water. Then partly paddling, partly wading and pushing, we made our way across. There were women squatting on the further shore, pounding dirty linen on the rocks at the water's edge. We hauled our possessions up the steep bank and found ourselves in the main street of the town. It was very broad, composed of hard, uneven mud, cracked into wide fissures in all directions and scored by several dry gulleys. On either side was a row of single-storied, whitewashed mud houses with tiled roofs; at each doorstep sat one or more of the citizens staring at us with eyes that were insolent, hostile and apathetic; a few naked children rolled about at their feet. The remains of an overhead electric cable hung loose from a row of crazy posts, or lay in coils and loops about the gutter.

The street rose to a slight hill and half-way up we came to the Benedictine Mission. This at any rate presented a more imposing aspect than anything I had seen since leaving Georgetown. It was built of concrete with a modestly ornamented façade, a row of unbroken glass windows, a carved front door with an electric bell, a balustraded verandah with concrete urns at either end; in front of it lay a strip of garden marked out into symmetrical beds with brick borders.

We approached rather diffidently for we were shabby and stained with travelling and lately unaccustomed to carved front doors and electric bells. But the bell need have caused us no misgiving for it was out of order. We pressed and waited and pressed again. Then a head appeared from a window and told us, in Portuguese, to knock. We knocked several times until the head reappeared; it was Teutonic in character, blond and slightly bald, wrinkled, with a prominent jaw and innocent eyes.

'The gentleman is a stranger too. He speaks Portuguese in a way I do not understand,' said David. 'He says there is a priest but that he is probably out.'

I was used to waiting by now, so we sat on the doorstep among our luggage until presently an emaciated young monk in white habit appeared up the garden path. He seemed to accept our arrival with resignation, opened the door and led us in to one of those rooms only found in religious houses, shuttered, stuffy and geometrically regular in arrangement; four stiff chairs ranged round four walls; devotional

86

oleographs symmetrically balanced; a table in the exact centre with an embroidered cloth and a pot of artificial flowers; everything showing by its high polish of cleanliness that nuns had been at work there.

The monk was a German-Swiss. We spoke in halting French and I explained my situation. He nodded gloomily and said that it was impossible to predict when another boat would leave for Manaos; on the other hand a new prior was expected some time soon and that boat must presumably return one day. Meanwhile I was at liberty to stay in the house if I chose.

'Will it be a question of days or weeks?'

'A question of weeks or months.'

David interposed in alternate Portuguese and English that he thought the Boundary Commission had a boat going down in a few days; he would go into the town and inquire. I explained to the monk that if this were the case I would gladly accept his invitation; if there were no Commission boat I would return with David to Guiana. With rather lugubrious courtesy the monk, who was named Father Alcuin, showed me a room and a shower bath; explained that he and the other guest had already breakfasted; sent across to the convent for food for me. I ate the first palatable meal since I had left St Ignatius, changed and slept. Presently David returned with reassuring information. The Commission boat was passing through in four or five days; a week after that there would be a trade launch. He smiled proudly both at bringing good news and because he had bought a startling new belt out of his wages. Then he and Francisco bade me goodbye and went to rest with the horses on the other bank of the river.

Already, in the few hours of my sojourn there, the Boa Vista of my imagination had come to grief. Gone; engulfed in an earthquake, uprooted by a tornado and tossed sky-high like chaff in the wind, scorched up with brimstone like Gomorrah, toppled over with trumpets like Jericho, ploughed like Carthage, bought, demolished and transported brick by brick to another continent as though it had taken the fancy of Mr Hearst; tall Troy was down. When I set out on a stroll of exploration, I no longer expected the city I had had in mind during the thirsty days of approach; the shady boulevards; kiosks for flowers and cigars and illustrated papers; the hotel terrace and the cafés; the baroque church built by seventeenth-century missionaries; the bastions of the old fort; the bandstand in the square, standing amidst fountains and flowering shrubs; the soft, slightly swaggering citizens, some uniformed and spurred, others with Southern elegance twirling little canes, bowing from the waist and raising boater hats, flicking with white gloves indiscernible particles of dust from their white linen spats; dark beauties languorous on balconies, or glancing over fans at the café tables. All that extravagant and highly improbable expectation had been obliterated like a sand castle beneath the encroaching tide.

Closer investigation did nothing to restore it. There was the broad main street up which we had come; two parallel, less important streets, and four or five more laid at right angles to them. At a quarter of a mile in every direction they petered out into straggling footpaths. They were all called 'Avenidas' and labelled with names of politicians of local significance. The town had been planned on an ambitious scale, spacious, rectangular, but most of the building lots were still unoccupied. There was one fair-sized store, a little larger and a little better stocked than Figuiredo's; half a dozen seedy little shops; an open booth advertising the services of a barber-surgeon who claimed to wave women's hair, extract teeth and cure venereal disease; a tumbledown house inhabited by the nuns, an open schoolhouse where a fever-stricken bearded teacher could be observed monotonously haranguing a huge class of listless little boys; a wireless office, and a cottage where they accepted letters for the post; there were two cafés; one on the main street was a little shed, selling *farine*, bananas and fish, there were three tables in front of it, under a tree, where a few people collected in the evening to drink coffee in the light of a single lantern; the second, in a side street, was more attractive. It had a concrete floor and a counter where one could buy cigarettes and nuts, there were dominoes for the use of habitués and, besides coffee, one could drink warm and expensive beer.

The only place, besides the Benedictine priory, which had any pretensions to magnificence was the church, a modern building painted in yellow and orange horizontal stripes, with ornate concrete mouldings; there were old bells outside, and inside three sumptuous altars, with embroidered frontals and veils, carved reredoses, large, highly coloured statues, artificial flowers and polished candlesticks, decorated wooden pews, a marble font bearing in enormous letters the name of the chief merchant of the town, a harmonium; everything very new, and clean as a hospital – not a hen or a pig in the building. I was curious to know by what benefaction this expensive church had come into being and was told that, like most things, it had started 'in the days of the Company'.

I discovered one English-speaking person in the town; a singularly charmless youth, the illegitimate son of a prominent Georgetown citizen whom I had met there at Christmas time. This served as a fragile link between us, for the young man told me that he hated his father and had thought of shooting him on more than one occasion. 'Now I have been married and have written five times for money and had no answer.'

He was completely fleshless like all the inhabitants of Boa Vista, with dank, black hair hanging over his eyes, which were of slightly lighter yellow than the rest of his face. He spoke in a melancholy drawl. He was almost the only person I saw doing any work in the whole town. He drove a motor launch for the store-keeper and owned a small blacksmith's shop where he made branding irons and mended guns. Most of the other inhabitants seemed to have no occupation of any kind, being caught up in the vicious circle of semi-starvation which makes people too apathetic to exert themselves for more. Perhaps they picked up a few casual wages during the flood season when boats ran from Manaos fairly frequently and the ranchers came in for stores and needed labour for shipping their cattle. All the time that I was there I scarcely saw anyone except the school teacher earn anything – or spend anything. Even in the café the majority of customers came to gossip and play dominoes and went away without ordering a cup of coffee. At some miles distant was a settlement of soldiers who brought a few shillings into the town; they were reservists bedded out with wives on small allotments. An aged town clerk presumably received some sort of wages; so no doubt did the itinerant government vet who appeared from time to time; so did the wireless operator and an official of villainous aspect called the 'Collector'. But the other thousand-odd inhabitants spent the day lying indoors in their hammocks and the evenings squatting on their doorsteps gossiping. Land was free, and, as the nuns proved, could produce excellent vegetables, but the diet of the town was *farine*, *tasso* and a little fish, all of which were of negligible cost. But it was far from being the carefree, idyllic improvidence one hears described of the South Sea Islands. Everyone looked ill and discontented. There was not a fat man or woman anywhere. The women, in fact, led an even drearier life than the men. They had no household possessions to care for, no cooking to do, they left their children to sprawl about the streets naked or in rags. They were pretty – very small and thin, small boned and with delicate features; a few of them took trouble with their appearance and put in an appearance at Mass on Sundays in light dresses, stockings and shoes, and cheap, gay combs in their hair.

From fragmentary and not altogether reliable sources I picked up a little of the history of Boa Vista. It was a melancholy record. The most patriotic Brazilian can find little to say in favour of the inhabitants of Amazonas; they are mostly descended from convicts, loosed there after their term of imprisonment, as the French loose their criminals in Cayenne, to make whatever sort of living they can in an inhospitable country. Practically all of them are of mixed Indian and Portuguese blood. There is no accurate census but a recent medical survey in the *Geographical Magazine* reports that they are dying out, families usually becoming sterile in three generations; alien immigrants, mostly German and Japanese are gradually pushing what is left of them up country; Boa Vista is their final halting place before extinction. The best of them go out into the ranches; the worst remain in the town.

They are naturally homicidal by inclination, and every man, however poor, carries arms; only the universal apathy keeps them from frequent bloodshed. There were no shootings while I was there; in fact there had not been one for several months, but I lived all the time in an atmosphere that was novel to me, where murder was always in the air. The German at the priory constantly slept with a loaded gun at his bedside and expressed the same surprise at seeing me going shopping without a revolver, as a Londoner might show if one went out without a hat; the blacksmith, partly no doubt owing to his avocation, spoke of little else; one of his main preoccupations was altering trigger springs so that they could be fired quick on the draw.

There was rarely a conviction for murder. The two most sensational trials of late years had both resulted in acquittals. One was the case of a young Britisher who had come across from Guiana, panning gold. He had no right there and one evening in the café tipsily expressed his willingness to shoot anyone who interfered with him. The boast was recognized as constituting provocation when, a few nights later, he was shot in the back and robbed while entering his house.

The other case was more remarkable. Two respected citizens, a Dr Zany and a Mr Homero Cruz, were sitting on a verandah talking, when a political opponent rode up and shot Dr Zany. His plea of innocence, when brought to trial, was that the whole thing had been a mistake; he had meant to kill Mr Cruz. The judges accepted the defence and brought in a verdict of death from misadventure. It was the first time in my life that I found myself in contact with a society in which murder was regarded as being as common and mildly regrettable as divorce in England; there was no glamour in it; I found it neither heroic nor horrifying; instead it seemed to spring from some species of arrested development.

The officials at Boa Vista live at so safe a distance from supervision, and are so badly paid, that inevitably they make what profits they can from bribes. Fortunately my meagre baggage and travel-torn appearance did not excite their cupidity. I heard several stories later of their extortion that were probably true. Twice lately British ranchers had come down by motor launch, in the flood season, to buy provisions. In each case the officer in charge had attempted to seize his boat under pretext that some regulation had been contravened, and the ranchers had had to make their escape by night, in one case under fire.

From time to time attempts have been made to raise the condition of the town. A little before the War a German appeared with ample capital and began buying cattle. He offered and paid a bigger price that the ranchers had ever before received; he fitted out a fleet of large motor launches to take the beasts down to market at Manaos, the scheme being that if he could organize a regular supply and get them down quickly and in good condition their value would compensate for the higher rate; he even sent a man across the border with a bag of sovereigns to buy cattle at Dadanawa. The project was perfectly sound financially and would have brought considerable advantage to the district, but it was destined to failure. Before the first convoy had reached the market, he had been shot and killed by an official whom he had neglected to bribe. The defence was that he had been shot while evading arrest on a charge of collecting turtles' eggs out of season. The murderer was exonerated and the boats never reappeared at Boa Vista.

A more recent enterprise had been that of 'the Company', so frequently referred to. I never learned the full story of this fiasco, for the Benedictines were deeply involved in it and I did not like to press the question at the priory. The blacksmith gravely assured me that the scandal had been so great that the Archbishop had been taken to Rome and imprisoned by the Pope. There certainly seemed to have been more than ordinary mismanagement of the affair. Father Alcuin never mentioned it except to say that things had not gone as well as they had hoped. So far as I could gather the facts are these.

A year or two ago, inflamed by charitable zeal, the wealthy Benedictines at Rio conceived the old plan of bringing prosperity and self-respect to Boa Vista. Geographically and politically the town held the key position to the whole, immense territory of the Northern Amazon tributaries. The monks saw that instead of its present position as a squalid camp of ramshackle cut-throats, it might be a thriving city, a beacon of culture illuminating the dark lands about it, a centre from which they could educate and evangelize the Indians, a place that might typify the now very dubious superiority of the civilized life. They imagined it, even, as a miniature ecclesiastical state where industry, commerce and government should be in the benevolent hands of the Church; a happy dream, glowing with possibilities of success to those imperfectly acquainted with the real character of Boa Vista.

Accordingly 'the Company' was launched, under the highest ecclesiastical patronage, financed by Benedictine money and managed by the brother of one of the hierarchy. The method by which the town was to be raised to prosperity was, again, sensible enough to anyone who expected normal working conditions. Instead of the cattle being transported to the slaughter-houses at Manaos, they were to be butchered on the spot and tinned. Cheap corned beef, it was assumed, would rapidly take the place of the unnourishing *tasso* and would provide a more valuable and more manageable export than live cattle. The factory would provide regular and remunerative employment to all in the district and, following the best tradition of big business, 'the Company' would also provide the necessaries and amusements on which their wages should be spent; the profits, rapidly circulating, would be used in public services. No one had any ulterior motive; the whole scheme was for the glory of God and the comfort of the people of the place. In Rio, on paper, it all seemed faultless. Operations were begun on a large scale.

The canning factory was built and installed with the best modern machinery; an electric plant was set up, providing the streets and the houses with light; a fine church, a hospital and a small school were built; there was soon to be a larger school, a priory and a convent; liberal wages were paid out; two hotels and a cinema opened; a refrigerator provided Boa Vista with the first ice it had ever seen. Everything seemed to be going admirably.

But the monks at Rio had reckoned without the deep-rooted local antagonism to anything godly or decent; a prejudice which at the moment was particularly inflamed by the unforeseen arrival of an irresponsible American with a rival scheme for improvement. His more ambitious proposal was to run a motor road and railway through the impassable bush that separated the town from Manaos, a project more or less equivalent in magnitude to the making of the Panama Canal. Finding that concessions had already been granted to the Benedictines which made his already impracticable railway legally impossible, he fell back on explaining to the inhabitants the great advantages of which they had been deprived, the higher wages he would have paid, the greater prosperity which he would have initiated. The citizens, naturally disposed to see a sinister purpose in any activity, however small, had already become suspicious of the great changes that were taking place. The American emphasized the foreign birth of most of the Order and the relationship between the manager of 'the Company' and the high ecclesiastic in Rio, with the result that by the time the monks and nuns reached their new home, they found everyone fairly convinced that a swindle was being perpetrated at their expense. It was only with difficulty and some danger that they succeeded in landing, being attacked with hostile demonstrations and showers of stones.

From then onwards everything went against the Benedictines, who were insulted and boycotted. The canning factory proved a failure; no one would use the ice – an unnatural, impermanent substance, typical of everything foreign; dishonest stuff that had lost half its weight even before you got it home – they didn't want the hospital, much preferring to sicken and die in their hammocks in the decent manner traditional to the place; no one paid his electric light bill and the plant had to be stopped. The priests went down with fever and, one by one, had to be sent back to Manaos. 'The Company' became bankrupt and all further work was stopped. No priory was built, no big school, no convent. At the time of my arrival things were at their lowest ebb. Father Alcuin was the last priest left and he was so ill that only supernatural heroism kept him at his work. Often he was only able to totter to the church to say his Mass and then retire to bed in high fever for the remainder of the day. The palatial house in which he was living was the building originally intended for the hospital. Its two big wards were now occupied by a carpenter engaged in making benches for the church, and a government vet who fitted up a laboratory there, which he used from time to time between his rounds of the ranches; he was investigating a prevalent form of paralysis in horses which he attributed to worms. Whatever minute flicker of good still survived in the town was preserved by the nuns, silent, devoted, indefatigable, who lived in appalling quarters near the river bank, kept a school for the handful of bourgeois daughters, and nursed a Negro and an aged diamond prospector who had arrived separately in a dying condition from up country and were in no mood to respect the prejudices of the town. It was, as I have said, the lowest point; a new prior was expected daily to reorganize things and set them to rights.

The priory – as the hospital was now called – was no exception to the rule formulated in the last chapter, that the religious are served by idiots. A single Indian boy of impenetrable stupidity looked after us. He had a round brown face and a constant, mirthless grin which revealed rows of sharply filed teeth. He giggled when observed and would, in occasional bursts of confidence, produce for inspection a grubby sheet of lined paper on which he had tried to copy an alphabet written for him by Father Alcuin. He was absolutely honest, and dazed with delight when, on leaving, I gave him a small tip. His chief duty was to fetch the meals from the convent kitchen, quarter of a mile away. They arrived cold and dusty, but with surprising regularity. He also rang the angelus and could always be found by the bell rope half an hour before the time, waiting for the clock hands to reach the appointed place. The rest of his day was spent in talking to a captive monkey that was tethered to a tree in the garden, or in gaping, hour after hour, at the jars of worms which filled the vet's laboratory.

The only other occupant of the house was the German who had first greeted our arrival; a man typical, except in his eccentricities, of the men of his race whom one encounters in remote places all over the globe; part of the great exodus of disillusioned soldiers and students that followed the defeat of 1918, from Germany and the German colonies. I have encountered them, wistful and denational-ized as Jews, in Abyssinia, Arabia and East Africa, and they make real to me some of the claptrap of Nazi patriotism.

Mr Steingler was not a particularly attractive man. I never discovered what he was doing in Boa Vista. He had a minute and unprofitable plantation up the River Uraricuera where he lived in complete solitude and, I gathered from his conversation, great privation. He spoke vaguely of business he had to do in the town and would often go shuffling off to gossip at the stores; he spoke of some mail he was expecting but when eventually the boat arrived from Manaos, there was nothing in it for him; he would sometimes announce his imminent departure, but always stayed on. He said he did not like to leave while Father Alcuin was so ill. The truth was I think that he could not bear to leave a place where there were people to talk to him in German; and he liked the food. He was a demonstratively greedy man and used to give great boyish whoops and guffaws of delight as he helped himself to the dishes, for at his farm, as he often explained, he had only *farine* and *tasso*.

It was only by slow degrees that he had come to his present condition. He had had a good job with a commercial firm in Manaos; then he had come to Boa Vista in the days of 'the Company'; then he had wandered off on his own up-country. It is possible that he was staying on at the priory because absolute destitution awaited him at his farm.

He was a firm atheist and did not disguise his contempt for the activities of his hosts. I tried to point out to him once that it was particularly fortunate for him that some people still had such curious notions – the nuns had nursed him through a grave illness the year before – but he said 'No, it is nonsense. It is only for children,' and of the new prior who was coming, 'No doubt it is a step in his career.'

His appearance was extremely odd, for he carried himself with the stiff back of any infantryman, while his loose sandals made him drag his feet in an incongruous manner when he walked. He wore a shiny and threadbare suit of blue serge, a 'boater' straw hat, a crumpled white collar and a narrow black tie. His ankles were bare and his sandals of his own manufacture. He invariably carried an absurd little ebony cane with a dented silver crook. We went to the café together most nights but he would seldom accept a drink, saying at first that he could not drink beer when it was not iced; later I realized it was because he could not afford it himself and in this one form would not take hospitality he could not return (a peculiarly irritating form of priggishness), so to cover his pride I used to invent reasons – that a boat was expected, that Father Alcuin was better, that it was my birthday – and then he would drink the warm beer with relish and laugh loudly at whatever was said.

We talked in a laborious mixture of French and English, of neither of which languages Mr Steingler had much command; indeed he seemed to be barely intelligible in any language; his fluent Portuguese seemed to cause endless misunderstandings at the café and even his German seemed to puzzle Father Alcuin. The difficulty lay chiefly in discovering which of his many languages Mr Steingler was trying to speak. Conversation at meals was always uneasy, for Father Alcuin knew no English and only the most formal French; most of the time he and Mr Steingler would stumble along in German, occasionally explaining some obscure point in Portuguese; then, feeling that I was being left out of things, they would attempt to draw me in. Mr Steingler would suddenly bow towards me, beam, and make curious animal sounds in the roof of his mouth.

Most of us, when speaking a foreign language, make some attempt to imitate the accents of the country; heaven knows, it is usually a pitiable attempt, bearing the most meagre and shadowy likeness to the true sounds, but at least it is an indication that we *are* speaking an alien tongue, a warning light to the listener to pay closer attention; a salute of formal courtesy, like the running up of the country's flag in a foreign port. Not so Mr Steingler who made no difference of any kind in his pronunciation whether he talked German or English, French or Portuguese. Moreover, he had, through prolonged dena-tionalization, largely forgotten from what languages his vocabulary derived, and would come out with such disconcerting questions as *'Comment dites-vous "manquer" en French?'*

As a rule Father Alcuin was too ill to eat; when he was in fever he kept to his room, but in the days of intermission he usually sat at table with us, drinking a little soup. I do not think he ever liked me much or understood what I was doing in his house, but he accepted my presence without complaint as he accepted all the other hardships of Boa Vista. He used to get a little outside news from the wireless operator and retail it to us; also alarming rumours such as that the unemployed were sacking London and that an unprecedented epidemic of influenza was killing off the French like flies. Only on the subject of Freemasons did he show any violent emotion. It is possible that they had taken some sinister hand in the fiasco of 'the Company', for the organization assumes forces in South America that would appal their respectable brothers in England.

Was it really true that the King of England was a Mason?

I replied that I thought he was.

'Is that how he became king? Did the Masons put him on the throne?'

'No, he is king by legal hereditary right.'

'Then how did the poor man fall into their power?'

It was useless to explain that English Masons were for the most part headmasters and generals with, as far as I knew, no criminal activities.

'That is what they say until they have you in their power. And the Prince of Wales, is he a Mason too? Is that why he does not marry? Do the Masons forbid it?'

I think he began to suspect me of secret Masonry after a time, in spite of my conscientious assistance at Sunday Mass.

The church was, considering the villainy of the place, surprisingly well attended; largely, I suppose, because the nasal singing of the girls' school provided the only kind of entertainment of the week. These children, shepherded to their places by the nuns, were dressed up in clean muslin veils and, the wealthier of them, long white cotton gloves; they wore innumerable medals and coloured ribbons and sashes, proclaiming their different degrees of piety. They sang sugary little vernacular hymns in tremulous, whining voices. They occupied the greater part of the church. Beside them were the elderly women in best dresses and clean stockings. What with this weekly blossoming of femininity and the concrete architectural ornaments of the building, the candles and the artificial flowers, Sunday Mass was the nearest thing to a pretty spectacle that Boa Vista provided, and the men assembled in fair numbers to enjoy it. They did not come into the church, for that is contrary to Brazilian etiquette, but they clustered in the porch, sauntering out occasionally to smoke a cigarette. The normal male costume of the town was a suit of artificial silk pyjamas, which many of the more elegant had washed weekly, so that on Sundays they carried themselves with an air of great refinement and caution. Some minutes before the Elevation they might be seen unfolding their handkerchiefs and spreading them on the bare boards of the floor; then, when the bell rang, they would delicately kneel on one knee, rise, shake out the handkerchief, refold it and tuck it away in the breast pocket. This, however, was the practice only of the most pious; the majority remained throughout propped against the walls, staring at the napes of the girls' necks. A priest told me that when he was new to the country he had remonstrated with the men, telling them that this was no fashion in which to hear Mass.

'We haven't come to hear Mass,' they had replied, fingering the revolver butts in their holsters. 'We're here to see you don't interfere with our women.'

No other event marked the passing of the days.

In a previous travel book I once remarked that I was bored for some days on a Congo river steamer. Not only did the reviewers take hold of this as a suitable text for their criticism, but I received a handful of cross letters from strangers saying, no doubt with good sense, that if travelling bored me I had far better stay at home and, anyway, give up writing about it; some suggested that it was, to them, the height of adventure to drift through the rain between featureless mangrove swamps and that it was an intolerable injustice that I, who could afford to do so, should not provide others with the romance I could not appreciate. So I will not repeat my mistake. I will not say I was bored in Boa Vista but merely remark that I found very little to occupy my time. There was an edition of Bossuet's sermons and a few lives of the saints in French for me to read; I could walk to the wireless office and learn that no news had been heard of the Boundary Commissioner's boat; I could visit the English-speaking blacksmith and watch him tinkering with antiquated automatic pistols. This young man would not come with me to the café on account of his having recently beaten the proprietor – an act of which he was inordinately proud, though it can have required no great courage since he was a very old man and slightly crippled. I could give bananas to the captive monkey and I could study the bottled worms in the laboratory; I could watch the carpenter, in his rare moments of industry, sawing up lengths of plank. There was really quite a number of things for me to do, but, in spite of them all, the days seemed to pass slowly.

The blacksmith, who knew all that was going on in the town, promised to tell me as soon as the Commissioner's boat was sighted, but it so happened that he forgot to do so, and I only learned from Mr Steingler, one morning after I had been six days in the priory, that it had arrived the previous evening and was due to leave in an hour; the Commissioner was at that moment at the wireless station. I hurried off to interview him. Things might have been less difficult if Father Alcuin had been able to accompany me but it was one of the days when he was down with fever. Alone I was able to make no impression. The Commissioner was an amicable little man, in high good humour at the prospect of a few days' leave in Manaos, but he flatly refused to have me in his boat. I cannot hold it against him. Everyone in that district is a potential fugitive from justice and he knew nothing of me except my dishevelled appearance and my suspicious anxiety to get away from Boa Vista. I showed my passport and letters of credit, but he was not impressed. I besought him to cable to Georgetown for my credentials, but he pointed out that it might take a week to get an answer. I offered him large wads of greasy notes. But he was not having any. He knew too much about foreigners who appeared alone and unexplained in the middle of Amazonas; the fact of my having money made me the more sinister. He smiled, patted my shoulder, gave me a cigarette, and sharp on time left without me.

I cannot hold it against him. I do not think that the British Commissioners would have done any more for a stray Brazilian. But it was in a despondent and rather desperate mood that I heard his boat chugging away out of sight down the Rio Branco.

From then onwards my only concern was to find some other means of getting away from Boa Vista. The trade boat of which David had spoken became increasingly elusive as I tried to pin its proprietor down to any definite statement of its date of departure. He was the manager of the chief store, a low-spirited young man named

Martinez. I went to see him every day to talk about it; he seemed glad of a chat but could hold out only the vaguest hopes for me. The boat had to arrive first. It should be on its way with the new prior; when it came, there would be time enough to discuss its departure. All sorts of things had to be considered – cargo, mail, other passengers. Day after day went by until all faith I had ever cherished in the trade boat slowly seeped away. Ordinary vexation at the delay began to give place to anxiety, for everyone in the town seemed to spend at least three days a week in fever, and I had no wish to catch it; the malaria of that district takes a peculiarly disagreeable and persistent form. It seemed to me a poor gamble to risk becoming semi-invalid for life for the dubious interest of a voyage down the Rio Branco. So I abandoned the idea of Manaos and decided to return to Guiana and visit Dadanawa.

This journey, so simple from British territory, where one was supported by the goodwill of the mission and the ranchers, presented endless difficulties from the other side. There was a large ranch, surviving from the days of 'the Company', which still belonged to the Benedictines, but, with the arrival of the prior imminent, Father Alcuin could not take the responsibility of hiring me horses. Mr Martinez said he could arrange it but days passed and no horses appeared. He found me a guide, however, in the person of a good-natured boy named Marco; he was fifteen or sixteen, in from the country, and had been hanging round the store for some weeks in search of employment; this youth, after a house-to-house inquiry lasting several days, eventually secured the hire of a horse for himself, belonging, as it turned out, to Mr Martinez and quartered at the ranch on the other side of the river. I still needed another horse – if possible, two – and provisions. Mr Martinez had some tins of sweet biscuit and sardines; another shop had two tins of sausage; the nuns made bread and cheese. These would comfortably take us the three days' ride to Dadanawa. Horses were still an unsolved difficulty when help came from an unexpected quarter.

Mr Steingler had hitherto listened apathetically to my complaints, merely remarking from time to time, '*Les peuples ici sont tous bêtes, tous sauvages; il faut toujours de patience,*' until one day the thought came to him that there might be something in it for him. He opened the subject cautiously, saying one evening that even if I secured a horse, it would be impossible to get a saddle; both were equally important. I agreed. He then went on to say that it so happened that he had a very good saddle himself, one that he would not readily part with to anyone, a particularly fine, new saddle of European workmanship, a rare and invaluable possession in a country like this. However, seeing my difficulty, and feeling the kinship that one European feels for another in a savage country, he was willing to part with it to me.

He took me to his room and dragged it out from under his bed. It was made on the English pattern but clearly of the most slipshod local workmanship; moreover it was of great age and in deplorable condition, half unsewn, with padding as hard as metal, every leather frayed and half worn through, several buckles missing. I asked him what he wanted for it.

Between European gentlemen, he said, it was impossible to bargain over money. He would call in a friend to make an assessment. The friend was the carpenter from the next room who was transparently in the racket up to his eyes. He turned over the saddle, praised it (embarrassing himself and Mr Steingler by inadvertently detaching another buckle while he spoke) and said that, all things, considered, 20,000 *reis* (£5) would be a moderate price. A new saddle, made on the ranches, with elaborate ornamental tooling, cost rather less than that in the country, but European gentlemen could not bargain over money. Besides I saw a possibility of advantage to myself. I accepted the assessment and then began in my turn, to point out that necessary as a saddle was, and much as I admired this particular one of Mr Steingler's, it was of very little use to me without a horse. I would buy it at his price, if he would find me a mount to put under it.

From that moment onwards Mr Steingler worked for me indefatigably. He set out there and then in his boater hat, twirling his ridiculous cane, and by evening was able to report that the Collector had the very horse for me; a beast of some age, he admitted, but immensely strong, big boned, well-conditioned; just what was needed for savannah travelling. We went to see him. He was of much the same quality as the saddle and curiously enough, commanded exactly the same price. Presumably 20,000 *reis* was a unit in their minds, the highest figure to which avarice could aspire. I bought him on the spot. I do not know what rake-off Mr Steingler got on the transaction, or whether he merely wished to keep in with the

Collector. I preferred to be thought a mug and get away, rather than to achieve a reputation for astuteness and risk spending an unnecessary hour in Boa Vista.

That evening Mr Steingler did a further bit of business by producing the town clerk, a venerable old man with a long white beard, who was willing to hire me a pack horse he owned in the corral on the further bank – 4,000 *reis* for the journey to Dadanawa. I paid him and went to bed well contented with the prospect of immediate escape.

Next morning I bade farewell to Father Alcuin. The plans for my departure had been freely discussed at table for over a week, but had not penetrated the feverish trance in which the poor monk lived. He was greatly surprised, and when I handed him a donation to the house to cover my board and lodging, he woke suddenly to the fact that he had exerted himself very little on my behalf; it was then that he revealed, what before he had kept carefully hidden, that he had a wooden pack saddle which he could put at my disposal. Thus equipped and blessed I felt that I was at last on my way.

But it was not to be as easy as that; the forces of chaos were still able to harass my retreat and inflict some damaging attacks. The next two days, in fact, were slapstick farce, raised at moments to the heights of fantasy by the long-awaited appearance of the prior.

News of his approach and imminent arrival came on the morning of the day that I had fixed for my departure. Instantly the priory was overrun by nuns. They worked in the way nuns have, which is at the same time subhuman and superhuman; poultry and angels curiously compounded in a fluttering, clucking, purposeful scurry of devoted industry; they beat up the prior's mattresses and dusted every crevice of his quarters, they trotted to and fro with wicker rocking-chairs and clean sheets, they lined the corridor to his room with potted shrubs, put palm leaves behind all the pictures, arranged embroidered tablecloths on every available shelf and ledge, decorated the bookcase with artificial flowers, built a triumphal arch over the front door and engrossed programmes for a hastily organized concert. I regretted very much that I should not be there to see his reception.

My plans were that I should cross the river in the afternoon with the grey cob I had bought from the Collector, see to the rounding in of the other two horses, sleep by the corral on the further side and start for Dadanawa first thing the next morning.

Mr Martinez had organized the crossing, for which he had hired me a canoe and another boy, whom I was to meet with Marco at three o'clock. At half-past four they arrived; the other boy turned out to be a child of eight or nine. Mr Martinez explained that he was taking the place of his elder brother who had fever that day.

We carried the saddles and baggage down the bank, found the canoe, which when loaded was dangerously low in the water. The descent at the usual landing place was too steep for a horse, so it was arranged that the small boy and I should paddle to a point upstream where the bank shelved down more gently, where Marco would meet us with the horse. It was half-past five when we reached the place and found no sign of Marco. The sun sets at six. For half an hour the small boy and I sat hunched in the canoe – I cramped and fretful, he idly playful with my belongings – then we paddled back in the darkness to the landing place. Sundry whistlings and catcalls ensued until presently Marco loomed up through the shadows riding the grey. We neither spoke a word of the other's language but by repetitions and gestures and that telepathy which seems to function between two people who have something of urgency to communicate, we got to understand that the horse had taken some catching, that Marco was quite ready to try swimming him across in the dark, that I thought this lunacy, that the baggage was to be left where it was, that Marco was to sling his hammock by the bank and guard it all night, that I could come at dawn and we would cross over then. I cannot explain how we discussed all this, but in the end the situation was well understood. Then I hurried back to the priory which I had left a few hours before with so many formal thanks and good wishes.

In my vexation I had entirely forgotten about the prior. I now came to the refectory, ten minutes late for dinner, out of breath and wet to the knees, to find him sitting at table. He was, as it happens, in the middle of the story of his own sufferings on the way up. It was a problem of good manners of the kind that are solved so astutely on the women's pages of the Sunday papers. What should I do? It was clearly impossible to escape unobserved, for the prior had already fixed me with a look of marked aversion. I could not slip into a chair with a murmured apology for my lateness, because some explanation of my reappearance was due to Father Alcuin and of my existence to my new host, the prior. There was nothing for it but to interrupt the prior's story with one of my own. He did not take it too kindly. Father Alcuin attempted to help me out, explaining rather lamely that I was an Englishman who had waited here on the way to Manaos.

Then what was I doing attempting to cross the Rio Branco in the dark? the prior demanded sternly.

I said I was on my way to Dadanawa.

'But Dadanawa is nowhere near Manaos.'

Clearly the whole thing seemed to him highly unsatisfactory and suspicious. However, with the charity of his Order he bade me sit down. The idiot boy removed the soup plates and the prior resumed his story. In honour of his arrival a fish course had been added to the dinner; nothing could have been less fortunate for he had lived on fish for the last ten days and on that particular sort of coarse and tasteless fish that was now offered him. He glared at it resentfully over his spectacles and ordered it to be removed. Mr Steingler watched it go with evident distress.

The prior was no doubt a very good man, but he did not add to the ease of the refectory. He was thoroughly exhausted by his journey and in no mood to bustle off to the nuns' concert. He had already formed a low opinion of Mr Steingler and my arrival confirmed him in his general disapproval. He was there on a mission of reorganization and Mr Steingler and myself were obviously the kind of thing that had to be investigated and cleaned up. He finished his narration of delays and discomforts, took a dislike against the pudding, and before Mr Steingler had nearly finished his first helping, rose to recite an immensely long grace. Then, with hostile adieux, stumped away grumbling to the celebrations at the school.

Next day at dawn I saw him on his way to Mass and he was more amicable. I bade him goodbye with renewed thanks and went down to the river. The small boy and Marco were there; the baggage was intact; after an hour's perilous and exhausting work we got the canoe and the horse across to the other side; the child paddled back and I settled down to wait until Marco had collected the other horses. The pack horse was easily identified by some *vaqueiros* who were waiting there. He was a wretched creature, down in the pasterns, but our baggage was very light and it seemed probable that he would get it to Dadanawa. Mr Martinez's horse could not be found. After two hours Marco returned, smiling and shrugging and shaking his head.

Back to Boa Vista once more. We had to wait until noon for a canoe. I arrived at the priory once more, a good quarter of an hour late for luncheon. The prior's doubts of my honesty became doubts of my sanity. Once more I made my adieux, repeating the same thanks with increased apologies. Mr Martinez, at last roused to activity, decided to accompany me himself to the other side and find the horse. He issued a number of peremptory orders which were lethargically obeyed. His motor launch was brought up, four or five men recruited, and a formidable expedition set out. After some hours, the horse was discovered straying some miles distant, lassoed and led in. Then a further disaster occurred. A large sow which had been nosing round the baggage for some time discovered a way in to the kit bag and ate the whole of the bread and cheese on which I had been counting as my main sustenance in the next few days.

Back to Boa Vista; back to the priory, just as they were finishing dinner. The prior now regarded me with undisguised despair. I was able, however, to buy another loaf and more cheese from the convent. Next morning, without further contact with my hosts, I slipped out of the priory and left Boa Vista for the last time in Mr Martinez's motor launch.

SIX

There was a fringe of palm about a mile from the corral, which in floodtime marked the river's edge, but before we had reached it the red roofs of Boa Vista were already out of view. Looking back and finding the town invisible, I felt myself freed from the dead weight that I had been carrying about with me all the blank, fourteen days of my sojourn, but the gaiety and inward radiance were of short duration, for the mist of frustration which had enveloped all my dealings with the place still hung about us and followed us like the clouds of cabouri fly for the whole of that journey.

The horses had looked discouraging from the start but I had learned, since the first day at Takama, to expect ill-looking animals and even to get fair service from them. These, however, were well below the second-class of savannah horses. The best of them was the grey cob I had bought from the Collector; he was old and lazy and disposed to lie down in protest when the saddle was put on his back, but he was in reasonable working condition. Later he developed a gall high on his back, but we were able to improvise a rope crupper, padded with rag under the tail, which held the saddle back from the place, so that sometimes ridden and sometimes loaded with the pack, he alone finished the journey with us. Marco's horse was young and weak and had not been out at grass long enough since his last bout of work, but the boy was light and rode him easily, so that at a slow pace he was good for some days. The town clerk's pack horse was hopeless. How hopeless we did not realize until at the fifth mile he went dead lame in the off fore. There was now no question of taking him to Dadanawa; the only problem was whether he could make the nearest ranch. We were more than half-way, so that it would have been useless to turn back. We lightened his pack to a negligible weight, dividing it between our two mounts (mine, of course, lying down in protest) and at walking pace dragged him painfully on across the savannah. We passed no water that day; every creek was a gulley of cracked mud; although we covered less than ten miles, we took over seven hours in doing it.

It would be tedious to describe the next two days in detail. Our first half was at a ranch where all the men were away on a round-up except an aged, one-eyed *vaqueiro*. Although only a few miles from Boa Vista, the people seemed of a different race. A stout lady received us hospitably and three or four daughters saw to our needs, bringing out coffee and chairs and giggling discreetly at us from the shadows. Marco had none of the debonair grace of David. He would hang back diffidently, afraid to enter and, since I had no means of communicating with them, my intercourse with our various hosts and hostesses was limited to smiles and bows. He was able to secure the loan of a horse, however, to replace the lame pack horse, which we turned into their corral to await his return. It took him and the one-eyed man three hours to find it, so that we had already lost the good hours of the morning before we resumed our travels. Altogether we had lost a full day's stage in the first twenty-four hours. This was a serious matter as we were carrying a minimum of supplies and the bread speedily became uneatable, carried as it was, in a canvas bag under the full blaze of the sun. Another thirsty, monotonous day brought us to a little out-station where a bearded man, bare to the waist but heavily armed, was cooking some fresh pork. We dined with him and slung our hammocks outside his hut. Next day in another six or seven hours we reached a ranch where a man with a face like El Greco's St Ignatius was making a pair of leggings. Martinez's horse was by now good for very little and this was our last chance of getting a remount before Dadanawa. I saw Marco tackling him on the question and after long discussion, it was evident that the request was being refused. However he brought us luncheon – the inevitable *farine* and *tasso* – and seemed to be genial enough. I expressed admiration of his leather work with various grimaces and nods. We had only a handful of biscuits left from our stores and one tin of sausage. I opened the tin, turned it out on a plate and offered it to our host. He refused, but while I ate, I noticed that he studied the plate with keen interest. I renewed the offer and this time he leant across, cut off a piece with his clasp knife and tasted it suspiciously. He liked it and finished the plate. Those sausages won us a horse, for after the meal he beckoned to Marco and I saw with delight that he had taken a lasso off its peg in the wall of the house. They went out together and returned in half an hour with a sturdy little skewball mare. Whenever we made a change of horses I took the best, gave Marco the second and put the pack, which now weighed barely sixty pounds, on to the most tired – this was by now the Collector's grey. With renewed vigour we set out again and late in the afternoon forded the Takutu and rode up on to British soil, at a place where a large creek flowed out.

At sunset we found an Indian hut. If things had gone better, we should have been already at Dadanawa, but there was two days' ride still before us. We had a few dusty biscuits and the vague hope of finding provisions among the Indians on the way. The house where we camped was empty of food except for a little sour milk and *farine*. It was no mere fastidious distaste that kept me from eating *farine*; I had found on the journey to Boa Vista that it made me ill; accordingly I ate the last of the biscuits and went to bed hungry and slightly anxious for the future.

Hope and good spirits returned at dawn next day. There had been no light in the hut the evening before so that I had not been able to look at the map or attempt to fix our position. Now I began to take in our surroundings. Neither the ford was marked nor any of the ranches on the Brazilian side; all I had to go by was the position of the creek and two large groups of bush-clad hills that lay immediately to the east of us. It came to me that these must be the Kanuku Mountains and the Kusads; our position lay midway between them, and the creek beside which we were camped must be the substantial river marked on the map as the Sauriwau. I verified this by asking the Indian, pointing to the creek and saying 'Sauriwau?' He nodded emphatically. In that case the reason was clear why we had taken so long in reaching the Takutu, for instead of striking dead east from Boa Vista in the direct line for Dadanawa, we had turned north and were a good forty miles out of our way. The cattle trail to Dadanawa, as marked on the map, ran by the Sauriwau and this no doubt explained Marco's divagation. On these calculations we were only twenty miles from St Ignatius. I had no particular reason for going to Dadanawa except the desire to visit the manager whom I had greatly liked in Georgetown and the curiosity of seeing the home in which old Melville had reigned. In our present position of short provisions and two exhausted horses, the obvious course was to make straight for my old host at St Ignatius. I was unable to explain my reasoning to Marco and the map meant nothing to him, but by pointing north and saying 'Ignatius' and 'Bon Success' I got him to understand the change of plan. He was puzzled but acquiescent, so leaving him to manage the pack, I set out ahead on the fresh horse, a clearly marked trail before me, the knowledge that it was impossible to miss the way if I kept between the Takutu and the Kanuku Mountains and the confident expectation of surprising Father Mather at his twelve o'clock breakfast.

The air was clear and cool and the horse stepped out vigorously. As I gradually rounded the spur of the hills on my right I watched them assume the contour that I seemed to know so well; the high dark line that I had seen day after day from St Ignatius. After an hour or so the path I was following narrowed to a single line and finally disappeared, but this did not greatly worry me. I knew my direction and sooner or later I should come upon the main trail once more, so I rode on from half-past six until half-past eleven without much concern; then I began to feel it was time I came upon some familiar landmarks. There was a village which Father Mather and I had visited on foot: that could not be far away. Some Indian huts, suddenly emerging from the screen of sandpaper trees, raised my hopes but when I approached them I realized they were not those I expected. I rode up to one of them and a few women scuttled inside at my approach. I tried to question them, pointing in the direction I was going and saying 'Ignatius' and 'Bon Success', but could get no indication of answer. At another hut a man leapt on his horse and cantered away at my approach. I rode on with some misgivings.

A line of hills had appeared on the horizon in front of me, presumably the Pakaraimas, and I reflected that I had never known them appear so close. The sun was now well up and the heat was overpowering; the horse had lost his freshness and could not be got out of a walk; the ground on all sides was the cruellest – dried marshland broken into hard hummocks – with no sign of a path anywhere; I had had no meal for twenty-four hours and felt suddenly dizzy. My fear was that I had ridden past the mission and should turn back south-west to find it. Marco, who had everything with him including my hammock, was some miles behind. It is easy in that district to pass within quarter of a mile of someone and not see him. Since I was off the trail, there was no probability of his picking me up if I stopped to wait.

The horse could go no further, so I dismounted and led him. The only reasonable plan seemed to be to make for the river, which must lie somewhere to my left; there at least we could get water and there, if anywhere, would be the landmarks I needed. So very painfully and unsteadily we began walking across the baked sedge. The horse pulled back from the halter and I was obliged to remount; he stumbled on, utterly beaten. It was one of the low spots of the journey. I had been given a medal of St Christopher before I left London. I felt that now, if ever, was the moment to invoke supernatural assistance. And it came. At that moment we reached water – a broad creek flowing east to west. When we had both drunk we started out again, slightly revivified, downstream; and there the real miracle occurred in the appearance of an Indian hut standing among palm trees a hundred yards in front. Outside was an old Wapishiana saddling an ox. I came up to him and made signs that I wanted to eat. 'Good morning,' he said. 'You hungry? Come inside, please.'

A child unsaddled the horse and took him down to water. I entered and sat on the Indian's hammock. Presently his wife brought me cassava bread, three eggs and half a roast bird about the size of a grouse. At first I was too exhausted to be surprised at my reception. After I had eaten all I was offered my mind felt clearer. The old man came in and said, 'Where you going?'

'St Ignatius.'

'Me going that way too. Going Bon Success to see Mr Teddy. Me work for Mr Teddy's father. Taking *bwi* (ox) there this afternoon.'

'Is it far?'

'Not far. Get there tomorrow.'

Then it began to break in on me that I was far further astray than I had thought. I still did not understand how. I pointed to the hills I had passed.

'But those are the Kanukus.'

'No, no, those Kanukus,' and he pointed to the blue line of mountains on the horizon ahead of me.

But I was too tired to discuss the question further. I lay back in the old man's hammock and shut my eyes, and it was then, in the hour's rest I took, half-awake and wholly exhausted, that I slowly turned over in my mind what had happened and realized that an hour before I had been in serious danger of being lost and that when I could go no further four fortunate events had coincided in a way that seemed unlikely to recur often on the normal theory of probability; one, that I had found a house at all at that particular spot in a sparsely inhabited region, secondly that it belonged to an Indian who understood English, thirdly that he should have food in his house† and fourthly, the oddest of all, that he should be going on the same road as I, on the same day – a journey which he probably did not make twice in five years.

The problem may be stated mathematically thus: *Suppose that this particular district is crossed, on an average, by two strangers a year; one in every two hundred Indians knows some English; one in every fifty Indian houses possesses surplus food; most Indians go to Bon Success once in every five years; there is one Indian house every fifteen miles; on February 21st, 1933, a stranger's horse gave out within quarter of a mile of an Indian house, whose owner spoke English, had food, and was that day setting out for Bon Success. When is this likely to recur* (supposing for the sake of calculation that all strangers' horses give out at some stage of the journey)? As I see it, there is a 1 : 182.5 chance that there will be a traveller on any given day; a 1 : 5,475 chance that his horse will stop within quarter of a mile either side of a house; a 1 : 1,095,000 chance that the particular inhabitant will speak English; a 1 : 54,750,000 chance that he will also have food – and so on. But I am no mathematician, and possibly the question is not as simple as it looks. Anyway, I prefer to regard the incident as a benevolent intervention of St Christopher's.

We set out at three that afternoon, the old Indian leading on his ox. He had with him a small boy who, in spite of their disparity of age, was apparently his son. This child rode my horse which, now refreshed, seemed well able to carry him. I was more than once humiliated to observe what far better value the Indians got from

† A state surprisingly uncommon. Indians usually eat all they have as soon as they get it.

their horses than I could; it was not due solely to their slighter weight but to the way they rode, sitting forward, balanced on the fork of their legs, swaying with each step, bare heels gently drumming the flanks, the leathers – or, more often, the loops of rope – let down to the full stretch and only the great toe hooked into the stirrup. Probably my stolid, armchair, English style of riding took more out of the animals than my weight and my heavy boots. In this case the child sat bare-back and the horse trotted along beside us as gaily as if he had been following free. I rode the little mare that had been intended for the boy.

In this fashion we struck up a fair pace to the north-east across thick grass land and presently came to the trail I had lost earlier in the day. Towards sunset we came to a belt of palm trees, a creek and, beyond them, a deserted house, and there astride the ruinous roof and signalling ecstatically to us was Marco. Up till then, for no very good reason, I had rather disliked the youth; now his genuine delight at my reappearance and the way in which he manifested it, seizing both my hands and grinning all over his ugly little face, established a cordiality which, though it could not develop greatly owing to my ignorance of Portuguese, persisted until he bade me farewell some days later, laden with the preposterous purchases for which he had exchanged his wages at Mr Figuiredo's. We made another rearrangement by which the Indian took my grey and put the packs on to his ox, and then rode on together until about two hours after dark when we reached the Sauriwau where I had supposed us to be camping the night before. (Incidentally the name on the map appeared to be wrong, for everyone spoke of it as Sawari Wau.)† There was a large village here, I learned later; in the darkness we could see only one camp fire. The inhabitants came out to greet us but they had no food for us or accommodation, so we camped in the open and set out again before dawn, without dinner or breakfast.

That day we followed the trail round the foot of the Kanuku

† The greater number of the Indian names on the map are incorrect, largely owing to the explorers having employed guides from tribes unfamiliar with the districts they were crossing. Also in many cases to misread notes. Even the famous Kaieteur Falls owe their name to a clerical error. It should be Kaieteuk, the *k* and *r* being similar in the handwriting of Mr Barrington Brown who discovered them. I have adopted the prevalent usages throughout.

Mountains which I had thought myself to be on the day before. By noon we reached Mr Gore's ranch. He was away but his Indian wife gave us food, of which I was by then in some need, and after resting there for the full heat of the afternoon, we reached St Ignatius before dark. The Indian and his son took payment for their help in the form of red cotton, fish hooks, a knife, a necklace and a highly coloured celluloid comb, and rode on to Bon Success.

Father Keary was at the mission revictualling for another tour. He was a tall, ex-army chaplain, with the eyes of a visionary, a large grizzled beard, an Irish brogue, a buoyant and hilarious manner. He set off towards the hills on the day after my arrival.

I stayed on with Father Mather, resting, reading Dickens, writing letters to England (all of which were delivered several weeks after my own return) and making plans for departure. I was reluctant to go back to the coast by my old route, both because it is always tedious to retrace one's steps and because I felt I had seen too much of horses and the cattle trail and not enough of the bush and the rivers, but the objections to every alternative seemed so cogent that laziness had almost impelled me to do so when Teddy Melville passed by with the report that owing to disease in the savannah, an embargo had been placed on all animals crossing at Kurupukari. I should have to go by foot from there to the Berbice. That decided me; if I had to walk, I would walk in a more interesting direction. There was a line over the Pakaraima Mountains to a village called Kurikabaru, which was the furthest point of the mission itinerary. Father Mather had once made the journey and Father Keary went there annually. From Kurikabaru it was no great distance to the Upper Potaro where Mr Winter, whom I had met in Georgetown, was working for diamonds; his claim was the furthest point of penetration from the Essequibo. The intervening district was crossed by the Roraima line, up which the Boundary Commission had had their stores carried the previous year, so that the trail was bound to be still easily traceable. Moreover it was the route followed by the Clementis on their journey some years back, which was described and roughly mapped in a copy of the *Geographical Journal*. One could take a horse and pack bullock for the first four days from St Ignatius; after that it would not be difficult to recruit droghers from village to village.

I could have done nothing without Father Mather, but with his help everything became smooth. It took some time, however, to make preparations – a guide had to be procured, animals brought in, stores packed; it was ten days before I was again on the move.

During this placid interlude it was inevitable that I should often reflect on the pains and compensations of the sort of life I was living, and was going to live for some weeks more, and to contrast them with the things that are written and spoken about it. There is room for a good deal of debunking of the subject. I do not mean of the delight of travel. That is a different question altogether, for it is a delight just as incommunicable as the love of home. I mean the opinion which one frequently meets that the greatest physical and mental well-being can be attained only in the wild parts of the world. We have all been shaken by it at one time or another. Perhaps we have been discussing architecture when a Voice, as though from another world, has broken in with, 'Well, the finest roof I ever want to see is my own tarpaulin, pitched in the bush beside my own camp fire, and the knowledge that there's not another human habitation within a hundred miles of it', or discussing food, and the Voice has said, 'I never enjoy anything so much as sitting down after a twenty-mile trek to a billycan full of cocoa and a freshly killed piece of hartebeest cooked in an old tobacco tin.' In an instant the conversation is destroyed; the little restaurant in the Dordogne, about which you were going to speak so lyrically, is left unsung, and in the awkward silence such interruptions cause, every heart begins to sink slightly and the suspicion grows whether perhaps all our ideas of good living are not a delusion and that perhaps these decisive people from the desert *do* really know more than we about our own business.

Well, I have spent long enough time in the wilds to call that particular bluff. There are a hundred excellent reasons for rough travelling, but good living is not one of them.

Lying at ease in the gallery at St Ignatius I began to tabulate some of the fallacies thus put forward.

For instance, *that one felt free*. On the contrary, there seemed no limit to the number of restrictions with which the 'open life' hampered one. Every personal possession became an encumbrance to be weighed and considered, as so many more pounds to transport; like a snowball growing into an avalanche, the difficulties accumulated; additional baggage meant additional labour, which in its turn required more rations and more labour to carry the rations. As for freedom of movement, there were before me at the moment two directions only in which it was possible to travel with any hope of arriving at a destination.

That one was untrammelled by convention. I have never understood this, for I seem to know quite a variety of people, of all kinds of interests and degrees of wealth, and none of them seems burdened by these conventions of civilization one hears so much about. If the cliché refers merely to personal appearance, is it really more onerous to wear a bowler hat than a topee, to shave in the morning than to spend half an hour, every evening, picking ticks off one's body? The toilet of the tropics, with all its hygienic precautions, is every bit as elaborate as dressing for dinner. Or if it is the strain of social intercourse, surely it is easier to remember the few rules of conduct in which one has been trained from the nursery than to adapt oneself to the unpredictable politenesses, the often nauseating hospitality, of savages?

That one eats with a gay appetite and sleeps with the imperturbable ease of infancy. Nonsense. Of course, after my Brazilian crossing I fell with particular relish on the bread and marmalade and eggs and fresh beef of the mission, but these things are always delicious everywhere. However hungry I was I found it difficult to swallow and impossible to digest the *farine* and *tasso* of the ranches. If anything, hunger makes one's sense of taste all the keener, so that one finds things disagreeable which one would at other times accept. It is worth noticing that children, the only people in civilization who are constantly hungry, are also the most fastidious and can only under the heaviest compulsion be made to eat things they dislike. There was only one commodity which I found enjoyable in camp which I should not normally have liked; strong, very sweet tea, made with condensed milk. As for sleep, I scarcely had a single good night in the open; exhaustion does not necessarily make for sleepiness; with one's whole body on fire with insect bites, one's face above the blanket cold in the wind, incessant animal noises on all sides, it was exceptional if one got two hours' unconsciousness on end.

I noted these down at the time, together with other fallacies, intending to make an article of them, but later I thought that perhaps I was stalking a tree and that fewer people than I supposed were taken in by that kind of boasting; and later I fell to wondering whether there were any pleasures I had found in that country which I had missed in Europe, and decided that there were two. The first was washing; not that I do not wash in Europe or that I find it distasteful, but that the mild pleasure derived from one's warm bath before dinner at home differs in kind rather than degree from the exquisite, almost ecstatic, experience of washing in the tropics after a long day's journey; it was as keen a physical sensation as I have ever known, excluding nothing, to sit on a *tacuba* across a fast-flowing mountain creek, dabble one's legs, knee-deep and pour calabash after calabash of cellar-cool water over one's head and shoulders, to lie full length on the polished rocks and let the stream flow over one, eddying and cascading; even to write about it brings back a faint tremor of that full exultation, the ripple and splash of the water, the sharp tang of the germicidal soap. It was a pleasure that was renewed nearly every day; a thing to remember and aspire towards, in the blind heat and dryness and disappointment of noon.

The other pleasure I discovered, oddly enough, was reading; or rather rediscovered, for I seem to recall having experienced some pleasure in this occupation as a child. But never since; I have read numerous books for various reasons – to acquire information, out of curiosity to see what they were like, out of politeness because I knew the author; I have dipped into most bestsellers to make up my mind whether they were justly or unjustly successful, and as soon as I knew, I have put them aside; I have raced through detective stories because the problems they set leave an itch for completion, an instinct of the kind that makes one wish to put things straight on the chimneypiece of a strange house; I have read books because I was being paid to review them; but I had not for ten years read a book for the mere pleasure of the process. At Father Mather's I began to read with this motive, and by good chance the books he had were just those which were meant to be read in that way, and when I left him I took away a copy of *Nicholas Nickleby* and read it with avid relish during the ensuing journey, bit by bit while the light lasted, grudging the night every hour of her splendour and the day its toil, which kept me from this new and exciting hobby.

Alas, both these pleasures have eluded me since I came back to Europe. I have read several books, for the old reasons and in the old way; I have taken numberless baths of all temperatures; but the rapture is gone, irrecapturable, except by great effort and at a long distance.

A guide was eventually found for me in one of the nearby villages, a plump docile Macushi named Eusebio, who pretended to a greater knowledge of English than he actually had and answered, 'Yes', to everything whether he had understood or not. He was remarkable for having no personal possessions of any sort, and his first act was to borrow a large part of his wages in advance to fit himself out with clothes, cup, plate, knife, tobacco, and a grey felt hat for the journey.

He was a soft young man and he did not travel well, but I promised him that, if he gave satisfaction, I would take him to Georgetown with me and this hope kept him going through the rough places.

Tireless to the last in his kindness, Father Mather supplied me with provisions from his own stores and supervised my packing, making coverings for the more perishable things, performing prodigies of dexterity with elastic bands and waterproof wrapping. I obtained *farine* and dried meat for the droghers' rations from Figuiredo; also gunpowder, caps and shot to supplement my Woolworth trinkets in the more remote villages where money does not run; also a curious substance in a flat tin, labelled Marmalade, which when opened proved to be a purplish glucose jelly of most disagreeable nature. David rounded up a pack ox and a strong little horse for the first days of the journey. Everything was ready by March 4th and early on the 5th we set out for Pirosha under an agreeably cloudy sky.

The trail was clear enough and, after giving a lead to the ox across the Mocu-Mocu creek, I rode on ahead, leaving Eusebio to follow at his own pace, which was leisurely and irregular, a poor two miles an hour, for the animal lumbered from side to side, browsing as he went.

The first two stages were along the way I had come, through Mr Hart's and Daguar's ranches, and should have been without incident had I not again gone astray and in this way involved myself in the heaviest day's ride I had yet made. It was the old nursery trouble of being 'too clever by half'. I had left soon after seven and by twelve should have been within a short distance of Harts', when there was a fork in the trail on the far side of a creek, two equally prominent tracks diverging. My natural inclination would have been to take the one on the left, and I should have been right; false ingenuity, however, supervened, for in the bed of the creek there were marks of motor tyres. I knew that Mr Hart's was the only car in the district, so I cast round and eventually picked up the tracks again on the right-hand road. I followed the tyres mile after mile, surprised at the length of the journey but confident that in the end they would lead me to the ranch; there were frequent divisions in the way and I began to enjoy the game of finding the faint impress of the treads in the hard earth, and to applaud my own perception. At two o'clock thatched roofs came into sight, but they were not those of the ranch; instead was a little Macushi village with the trail leading through it and beyond to the horizon.

The headman came out to meet me. He knew no English and had no food, but he was able to point out my way to me. I rested for half an hour, and to entertain me, he produced a basket full of carefully folded spills of paper. These – unreadable, of course, to him – were all the documents that had come to the village from time to time: marriage licences from passing missionaries, a writ to someone to appear at court at Annai, several gun licences and an illuminated confirmation card – all charms of mysterious potency, paternally stored away in the eaves of his hut.

I rode back, at an acute angle from the way I had come, and finally reached Hart's at half-past five; the little horse, which had covered a good forty miles, trotted bravely to the last. I had supposed that Eusebio would be there before me and there might be some concern at my disappearance, but the Harts had seen nothing of him. While I was gratefully eating cheese and drinking tea they explained the mistake I had made. I had been within a mile of the house when I had followed the car tracks, made in a recent direct journey with government stores between Yupukarri and Bon Success.

Eusebio turned up at eight o'clock, having delayed on the road to cook and devour an armadillo which he had caught.

I thought that the horse could do with a day's rest so sent Eusebio ahead to Daguars' and spent another night at Hart's. Mr Hart was at home this time, a kindly, middle-aged American of wide experience, whose heart was more in woodwork than in cattle. In the evening I participated in a scene of curiously patriarchal piety; Mr Hart assembled the whole household, including sleepy children, the Creole governess like Josephine Baker and the old Wapishiana grandmother, and together we walked up and down in the moonlight, loudly reciting the rosary, Mr Hart calling on each of us in turn to lead the devotions. It was a performance which in normal surroundings would have paralysed me with shyness, but here it was not embarrassing, for the oddness of the company and the moonlit landscape made the occurrence half real and impersonal.

After Daguars', which I reached without misadventure at noon the next day, the journey entered on another phase. So far it had been increasingly strange and slightly more adventurous each week. The road I was now starting on promised to be by far the most interesting. It ran, very roughly, parallel with the Ireng, along the west of the Pakaraima Mountains, passing first through fairly well populated Macushi country, then through an uninhabited hinterland and then to the villages of the Patamonas; then, turning east, there was another empty stretch until I should strike Mr Winter's camp, who was prospecting somewhere in the upper Potaro district. Except Father Keary, on his annual round, no European or coast Creoles ever normally went into this country. A fair number of the men worked or had worked from time to time for Europeans, either collecting ballata or, less commonly, acting as droghers, but the villages themselves were untouched by civilization except at second or third hand. The line of communication to Roraima temporarily established by the Boundary Commission a year before had provided more work than usual, and in consequence there was a momentary glut of cheap hardware and Japanese cotton which gave some appearance of sophistication, but these perishable luxuries are no doubt already disappearing and the communities reverting to their primitive character, which was only very superficially disturbed.

Daguar was able to find me a mounted Indian to act as guide, so I sent Eusebio off that day to sleep on the road and meet me at Karasabai, the first village.

I had ridden to Daguars' with Teddy Melville, who was on his way from Hart's to Annai. We stopped on the way at a ranch I had always thought of as Marie Louise's but which I found was really Manoel Luiz's; this Brazilian Negro had at great age recently married a Portuguese girl from Georgetown and had, in her honour, repainted the front of his house so that it resembled a circus booth, with Union Jacks, heads of oxen and ill-counterfeited marble. He urged us to stay to breakfast, but I remembered the cooking at Daguars' and insisted on going on, where we were rewarded with fresh pork stewed in milk. We rested, in some discomfort from cabouri flies, until, with nightfall, they disappeared. Next day the guide and I set out for the hills.

From now onwards the government map, which had at the best of times been barely adequate, became quite without value, nothing on it except the course of the Ireng having any relation to the lie of the country. The trail wound in and out through belts of bush, across dry creeks, round patches of swamp and up narrow hill passes; its general direction was north-east for the first ten miles or so and then, sharply turning, north-west for another ten. At first I was fired with the ambition of making a compass traverse of the route and stopped to note every change of direction and topographical feature and to check our ascent with an aneroid, but I found the conditions so diverse and the way so intricate that I abandoned the project after a day or two. While it lasted, however, the practice made me observant of the country as I had not been before and heightened my enjoyment of the change of scenery. That, now I advert to it, should certainly be included with washing and reading as one of the delights of this journey. In Europe, with modern communications, you take it as a matter of course as you accept the shifting of canvas trees between the acts of a pantomime; you fall into a doze, while monotonous fields of stubble swim past the carriage window, and wake up amid lakes and mountains, or else you travel by aeroplane when all scenery is meaningless as a page from an atlas, as flat and as conventionally coloured, while between you and it lie fathoms of air and sunlight. But here every change was achieved by effort. I have already remarked on the Tartarean plunge on entering the forest and of the bird-like sense of liberation on leaving it. Now I found myself in the greatest transition of all, the emergence from monotony to change. For weeks I had seen nothing but savannah, sometimes a horizon of hills further away or nearer, but day after day the same road across absolutely flat plain, the same dun dapple of earth and grass, the whiter ruts of the cattle trail, the coffering of dried sedge, squat sandpaper trees or tattered, spinsterish palms. From now onwards the way was kaleidoscopic. Each of the number-less turns of the path, each emergence from bush disclosed a new spectacle, sometimes a dozen hill tops like the domes of Istanbul, sometimes a bare precipice of grass, a wooded channel, a rocky ascent, a black wall of forest, a grassy saucer sheltering a cluster of huts, a horseshoe of odd, conical hills, the glitter and black shadow of water as a loop of Ireng appeared suddenly at one's feet or a mountain stream tumbling to join it in a cataract over the smooth rocks – all negligible enough from a train window, but stimulating at a time when some encouragement was particularly valuable to get one on from one point to the next.

Except for one sharp ascent among rocks and loose pebbles where we dismounted and led our horses, we were able to ride all the way from Daguars' to Karasabai, making good time. In something less than four hours we came to a spur from which we could see a wide panorama of hill country, the Ireng, dark and menacing, far away to the left and, immediately below us to the right, the village of Karasabai. We crossed the Yurore creek and arrived just as Eusebio was unsaddling the pack ox. The village stood half-way up a large grass-covered valley lying north and south, encircled on three sides by high hills – a stadium more than an amphitheatre, for it ran back to some depth. To the north the hills were covered in bush, on the other sides bare. There were ten huts together and three roofs visible at a distance; one house stood on piles with a ladder leading to its door, the others were square, single-roomed structures of wattle and thatch of the sort I had seen all over the savannah. Eusebio had already found quarters for us in one of them; there was a little corral with a wooden paling enclosing some cows and half a dozen calves; there was also a long mud house, kept empty and used as a church when Father Keary visited the place. Eusebio told me that he was on the same road as us, had slept there the night before and that we should meet him at Tipuru the next day.

The chief man of the place offered me formal hospitality in the shape of *cassiri* in a tin bowl of European manufacture. I put it to my lips and passed it on to Eusebio. *Cassiri* is the drink of the country from time immemorial.† (It is curious how propagandists always talk as though alcohol had been introduced to the backward races by principled traders and imperialists, referring ironically to the joint import of gin and hymn books. In point of fact almost every

† There is also another similar drink named *piwari*.

race had discovered it for themselves centuries before European explorers appeared on the scene at all and used it on a large scale for frequent, prolonged orgies, besides which the most ambitious American parties appear austerely temperate.) It is made from sweet cassava roots, chewed up by the elder members of the community and spat into a bowl. The saliva starts fermentation, and the result is a thick, pinkish liquor of mildly intoxicating property. I was a little sceptical about the orgiastic nature of the ceremonial *cassiri* parties until I saw the vat in which it is kept. There is one or more in every village, according to its size. There were two at Karasabai in the back of the hut where we were quartered, and I took them at first to be boats, for they consisted – like most of the craft on those rivers – of entire tree trunks hollowed out. Before a party – and Father Keary told me with regret that the tendency was for the parties to become more frequent – the whole village chews and spits indefatigably until the vat or vats are completely full. Then, after the fermentation has been under way for some time, they all assemble and drink the entire quantity. It usually takes some days, beginning sombrely like all Indian functions, warming up to dancing and courtship and ending with the whole village insensibly drunk.

The people crowded out to greet us, one by one presenting themselves and shaking hands with shy manners and downcast eyes; then they formed a close circle and stared from noon until sunset without intermission. When one looked directly at them they looked away but immediately resumed their emotionless scrutiny when one was occupied elsewhere. They were not hostile or amused or, it seemed, particularly observant; they stared as yokels stare over gates. They watched every object unpacked without apparent curiosity; when I left the open hut none of them attempted to touch the baggage or play with it, as they would have done in most parts of Africa. The only thing which moved them was my camera from which they fled in alarm. They were all unattractive, squat and dingy, with none of the grace one expects in savages. They seemed to have singularly little interest in personal adornment. Their hair was lank and ragged with none of the ochre powder, bone combs and skewers, the high, architectural coiffes, poodle-like shavings, beloved by the African. A few had lines and spots of blue tattooing on the face but none of the intricate incised and embossed ornament, the monstrous structural operations to nose, lips and ears, the backs and breasts scarred and pitted in pattern like Venetian leatherwork, that makes Negro beauty so formidable to a newcomer. Most of them had a hole pierced in the lower lip, stuck with a quill or piece of wood. Each had a necklace on which was strung his *bena* (a charm consisting usually of some part of an animal – tooth or bone), the religious medal he was given at baptism and a miscellaneous collection of things that had taken his or her fancy – nuts, teeth, beads, buttons, coins, gun-caps; the women had the lower part of the leg, below the knee and above the ankle, tightly bandaged with fibre or beads to swell out the calf, which is regarded as a centre of attraction in this country as are the breasts in Europe, the feet in China and the buttocks in most parts of Africa. A few of the men, those that had recently been out to work, wore shorts and vests but most of them were naked except for the *lap*, a red cotton loin cloth; the women, without exception, had soiled, colourless dresses.

These I learned were only worn in the presence of strangers. In her own village – which practically means her family, for the community is inextricably interrelated – an Indian woman goes naked except for a little bead apron six or seven inches square. Often when approaching a village I used to see the women scurry into their houses and emerge clothed; only very rarely did they appear in front of me or the droghers – for an Indian from another tribe or even another village is a stranger every bit as alarming as a white man – without their dresses and when they did so it was because they were poor and had no stuff, not because they were less modest. Still less was it because they were less Christianized.

That is another complaint of propagandists, that the Christian missionaries teach the natives to be ashamed of their bodies and, by distributing petticoats, deprive them of all the moral and hygienic advantages of nudism. There may be some truth in this legend somewhere. I have read accounts of the activities of American Baptists in the South Seas that seem to support it, but as far as my personal experience goes I have found the reverse to be true. I have talked to Dutch, French, German and English missionaries, Protestant and Catholic, in widely different parts of the world and found them either indifferent or mildly opposed to the clothing of their converts. If they give them clothes, it is because they know it is the most welcome present they can offer, for the truth is not that dresses are forced upon them, but that the moment they have set eyes on a fully dressed woman most savages will as readily give their love to the trader as their souls to the missionary in order to imitate her; if petticoats are going at the mission house, she will be baptized, confirmed, taught the story of Noah's Ark or the Ten Commandments to get one, for clothing appeals equally to the two usually contradictory instincts of modesty and ostentation. In the case of the Guiana Indians, with exception of those like the hostess at Daguars' who have become definitely civilized, the motive seems to be entirely modesty. They have a shrinking from anything that makes them obtrusive. They wore their grubby linen without any of the swagger and provocation of a Negress, for it was no adornment, merely a shield between them and an alien world.

Eusebio reported that there were no supplies to be got in the village, Father Keary's party having exhausted whatever there had been, so I breakfasted off biscuits, sardines and tea. My audience never left me but I soon grew used to their presence and was able to wash, eat, write or sleep without regard to them. In the late afternoon I strolled round the village, followed at a short distance by most of the inhabitants. There were several women suckling children, two weaving hammocks, another spinning cotton on a little hand bobbin; a man was mending a blow-pipe. I had read about these weapons in detective stories and had imagined them – as obviously had the authors – as short instruments easily concealed about the person. This one was about eight foot long; the dart they use is the size of a pen – I had imagined a barely visible thorn – but it is true that they shoot with amazing accuracy. It is also true that the Indians have the secret of the 'deadly vegetable poison which defies analysis' that appears so often in the more old-fashioned shocker, but the difficulty of obtaining the poison is gradually driving the blow-pipe out of use. Various explorers from time to time have obtained bits of the poison and recipes for its concoction but none, I think, have proved genuine; they usually contain numerous magical ingredients such as ants and scorpions, but the bases are without doubt certain obscure plants which the Indians take pains to hide. If, in some exceptional moment of indiscretion, they give a name, the inquirer is little the wiser, for it is one unknown to botany and the secret of its location is never divulged. There are, of course, numerous common plants that are poisonous and are openly used for polluting streams for fishing but there is more than one that the Indians know about and will not reveal. None of them are common but it is handed down orally among the *piai* men where they can be found. Father Keary once encountered a party of his converts on a journey many days from their village. He asked them what they were doing and they at first demurred; finally they confessed that they were on an expedition to collect a certain bark with which to make away with an unpopular man in their community. He induced them to turn back but he never learned what the tree was or where it grew. Reliable authorities who have seen the arrow poison in use describe it as a dark paste, a minute portion of which in an open wound causes immediate paralysis and death. There is said to be another poison which causes insanity but the evidence for this is less conclusive. The general tendency since the introduction of firearms seems to be for poison to go out of favour among hunters and to be confined solely to the use of homicides and fishermen.

At one house a man lay in his hammock, apparently in the best of health but being attended with all the circumstances of illness. A woman with a very small baby at her breast was holding a calabash to his lips for him to drink. I asked Eusebio what was the matter and he explained that the man's wife had lately given birth to a child. I had read about this convention and heard it spoken of by Father Mather and the ranchers. It is prevalent among most of the tribes of the country, particularly the Wapishiana, and forms a curious contrast to the views on procreation taken in other equally savage parts of the world.

Here, as among most primitive peoples, parturition is a comparatively easy process; a few hours before it and a few hours after the mother will be sturdily trotting about seeing to the business of the home. The father, on the other hand, is laid up for some weeks, keeps to his hammock, is tenderly nursed and receives the congratulations and sympathy of his relatives and neighbours. The explanation given by those anthropologists who have noticed the practice is that the soul of the child is linked with the father's so that while it is in the precarious stage of early infancy any risk he takes may endanger it. That is purely a hypothesis because, of course, the Indians have neither the vocabulary nor inclination for metaphysical discussion. The fact, however, is indisputable, and it is interesting as forming a contrast to another anthropological hypothesis which became popular on the publication some years ago, of Professor Malinowski's *The Sexual Life of Savages*. That book, well written and superbly illustrated, enjoyed a success far beyond the ordinary public of anthropological students. It dealt with a universally absorbing subject and it printed love songs which general readers found agreeably indelicate. It treated, conscientiously and brilliantly, of one group of savages, the Trobriand Islanders, and described, among many other significant things, how they had no knowledge at all of the paternal contribution to procreation. The hypothesis based on this was the familiar one, that man has evolved his social organization from a matriarchal herd. Now partly because, as I have said, the book found its way to unsophisticated readers and partly because its title was *The Sexual Life of Savages* in general rather than of *Trobriand Islanders* in particular, countless 'Outline'-educated people jumped at the belief that the Trobriand Islanders' ignorance was universal to primitive man and the herd hypothesis established.

Of course, anthropologists are no more unprejudiced than any other scientist – or any amateur observer like myself. Most work in that field comes either from inquirers, flushed with the agnosticism of the provincial universities and firmly convinced beforehand that man's idea of God and right conduct have evolved from the vague speculations of an animistic, matriarchal herd, or from missionaries fresh from their seminaries, equally well convinced that man is descended from a single monogamous, monotheistic pair, and that when erroneous beliefs are prevalent it is because people have deteriorated with the ages and muddled and forgotten what was once a clear, revealed fact. Both parties jump at any peculiarity that seems to support their views. When Christian anthropologists discovered that the temptation of Adam and Eve by the serpent in the Garden of Eden was a myth widely held outside the Jewish nation, they pointed to that fact as proving that, since all were descended from Adam and Eve, all had the tradition of their origin though only the Jews had been enabled to keep it completely free from contamination; the other party, less logically but no less triumphantly, said that it proved that Genesis was not an inspired book if people who had not read it believed what it told. I have met ecclesiastics who maintained that the widespread dislike of snakes and the peculiar prominence given them above all other creatures in many cults was also a product of the Garden of Eden tradition.

However that may be, it seems worth pointing out for what it is worth that the ideas of parental responsibility of the primitive Guiana Indians† are the direct opposite of those of the Trobriand Islanders, and that no theory based on the latter can neglect consideration of the former.

My guide from the savannah would go no further, but Eusebio found me another mounted Indian, so that next morning I was again able to ride on ahead and leave him to follow with the ox. We started half an hour after dawn and rode up the valley to where, in its north-east, it narrowed into a defile. It was marshy at the top and there was a creek to ford. Some bush closed in round us but the trail was clear and we could keep up a steady trot; there were open patches, but for the most part that day's journey was through bush, up a series of little passes, climbing all the time, occasionally so sharply that we had to dismount. We passed an Indian family on the trail, the men in front armed with bows and arrows, the women behind carrying the luggage. Once the way opened into a wide valley, wooded on all sides but grass at the bottom and in the centre of it, two knolls, one crowned by a hamlet of three round houses. At eleven o'clock we left the bush and came into downland, successive crests of low, grass-covered waves with the trail clearly marked across them. Another half-hour's bush ride brought us to Tipuru.

It was a particularly attractive place, built on the summit of one of the little hills, where an outcrop of rock broke through the grass, and extending down one side of it towards the stream after which it was named. The houses were substantially built and so compact together that the trodden earth between them had almost the nature of village streets. At Karasabai the houses had mostly been open on three sides, but here the mud walls were built up into the eaves to keep out cabouri fly and the interiors were dark and warm. The mission owned a house and a church in the village and some cows in the corral, for this was an important village, both by reason of its size and its position, which made it the terminus beyond which horses and pack animals could not be taken and consequently the

† The Guiana Indians as far as is known never participated at all, or had any contact with, the high civilization of the Indians in medieval Peru.

recruiting place for droghers on the long march in the mountains. Here too the people from the outlying hamlets could assemble if they had children to baptize – for hazy as most of the Indians may be on the more elaborate truths of Christianity, they are all keen for baptism. The head man – chief is too large a term – was a fine-looking old man, unique among all the Indians I saw in the possession of a stubble of grey beard.

When Father Keary's surprise at my arrival had somewhat abated, we breakfasted together in the hut reserved for him. His presence made everything a great deal easier for me, for now I was able to entrust the horse and pack ox to the men he was sending back to St Ignatius; he would also be able to help me collect droghers, a process over which I had anticipated considerable difficulty. That afternoon, after he had spent an hour in the church teaching the children the rosary in Macushi, we went round the village but even with Father Keary's help and his head boy, Antonio, we found droghers difficult to procure. The Indian men do not like carrying loads, regarding it as women's work, and the women will not travel without their men, so that one was obliged to engage and feed and carry the rations for twice the labour one required. I also needed a hunter and no one in the village seemed to possess arms, so that after two hours' laborious negotiations it looked as though the journey would not be possible, at any rate until we had sent into the surrounding country for additional help.

It was then that Father Keary proposed that we should combine our expeditions. He had in any case to go two-thirds of the way in the same direction; his original intention was to spend three or four days in each village, but he could easily, he said, travel straight through and make longer visits on his return journey; moreover the country between the last of his villages and Mr Winter's camp was unknown to him and he would like the opportunity to explore it. I agreed eagerly and so it was arranged. To help with our provisions Father Keary ordered a cow to be slaughtered.

This was all that was needed to overfill the cup of local excitement. The tension, apparent all through the afternoon, at last snapped. Two white men had arrived in two days, each with strange Indians, and now a cow was to be killed. Blank little Mongolian faces creased noticeably at the corners of the eyes and mouth in expressions of, to them, wild emotion. The meat was chopped up, salted and packed, and the offal distributed. In an hour everyone in the place from the smallest children to the oldest grandparents, had possessed himself of a handful of steaming entrails and was trotting to and fro, in and out of the houses talking in a manner that would have been extremely morose in any other country in the world, but here was an almost hysterical outburst of animation.

While the village were feasting that night, Antonio told us a curious story, that there were skulls and bones hidden among the rocks about quarter of a mile away. He had not seen them himself, nor had anyone whom he knew, but it was certain they were there. He did not know how long they had been there, but threw his head back and made the inevitable whining noise by which an Indian conveys distance, in time or space, greater than he can compute. They were the bones, he said, of Arakuna Indians from whom the Macushis had taken the village generations ago.

It was an odd story, new to Father Keary and contrary to what is generally held about these hill Indians, that they have no military traditions. It was the only time that Antonio ever volunteered information or told us any but the most practical and generally inaccurate details of the distances and directions of streams and camping places. It is possible he was moved to boast by pride in his own village and wished to explain that it was different from the others. Usually if one asked him anything about the beliefs or habits of his people he would look away and, perhaps, snigger.

SEVEN

On foot in the hills – cabouri fly – *Kenaima* – Karto – *djiggas* – Kurikabaru –
Santa Maria – Anundabaru – Mr Winter – base treatment of Eusebio

We set out on foot next morning across the Tipuru, walking one
behind the other in a single file which presently spaced out until we
straggled a good half-mile from first to last. The organization was
in Father Keary's hands and I had been witness to some of the
difficulties that attended it, so I was not critical; there did seem,
however, to be more people in our party than our needs warranted.
First there was a sturdy gnome-like woman of great age, who, since
she was a slow walker, always set off alone an hour before the rest
of the party, was passed half-way and finished a constant but
undismayed last. She carried nothing except her own belongings, a
slab of meat, and a few cooking pots; her interest in coming seemed
to be change of air, healthy exercise and the pleasure of observing
two foreigners in discomfort; also the half-dollar a day in trade goods,
which she received in common with the more heavily burdened
members of the expedition. Then followed Antonio who as guide
and interpreter was too proud to carry anything except a gun and
a cutlass; behind him plodded his wife bowed double with his
luggage, her own, and a fair share of the general rations; she was
one of the few attractive Macushi women I saw, stocky and drab
but with a very sweet, childlike face and long loose hair which blew
round her head on the hill tops. Then came Father Keary and
myself, and behind four other droghers and Eusebio. He showed a
clear aversion to taking a load and usually escaped without anything
heavier than the things I needed on the road – hammock, towel,
change of clothes, rations for the next meal, and the rapidly depleted
bottle of Lisbon brandy which I had bought from Figuiredo. Even
so he started reluctantly, looked pathetic all day and often ended

only a few paces ahead of the old woman. The heavy stuff, Father Keary's altar equipment and the *farine* rations, were borne by two brothers, very large and muscular for their race, shock-headed, with lowering cave-man brows and loud, unexpected laughs; they were more untamed than their companions, whom they seemed to despise, and ate apart from them.

They all went barefoot except over the rocks when they would produce flat sandals of palm bark. Father Keary and I wore rubber-soled canvas boots. There is no satisfactory alternative to my knowledge, for we were in a country where one is wading streams five or six times a day and then rapidly becoming dry in direct tropical sun, but the softness of the soles, though it prevented blistering to some extent, made the feet easily bruised on loose stones and the trellis of root in the bush.

We walked for about five hours with a ten-minute rest half-way at a village of five houses named Shimai, and finally made camp by the Maripakuru creek, a short distance from its confluence with the Ireng; there we found a solitary skeleton house, half-built and then deserted, and slung our hammocks under the thatched section of its roof. Our day's progress seemed discouraging for the trail had wound in and out of the bush, up creeks to find suitable fords, over steep passes and round spurs, climbing all the way, so that though we had covered a lot of ground and were thoroughly tired, our actual distance from Tipuru seemed negligible.

The cabouri fly here were unbearable so that though we wrapped our hands in handkerchiefs – gloves were one of the highly desirable things it had not occurred to me to bring – and swathed our necks and faces in towels, there was no sleep and little real rest until sunset. We had no lamp with us, so it was necessary to eat by daylight, and even the small amount of uncovering necessary to enable us to swallow and to handle spoon and knife, made meals, hungry as we were, wholly unwelcome. The bath was delicious so long as one remained submerged, but any limb that appeared over the surface of the water was instantly covered with voracious flies. Cabouri will not attack one so long as one is in motion, and I found it on the whole more agreeable to walk up and down, in spite of stiffness and soreness of feet, than to lie tormented in the hammock. Antonio went out with his gun but came back empty-handed, but we still had fresh meat from the kill at Tipuru so this did not worry us. The truth became clear later, when we were in some need of food, that he was a thoroughly incompetent hunter; moreover, the moment he was out of his own country he became timid, and made excuses to avoid leaving the party.

The life of every Indian in these parts is overshadowed by an ever-present, indefinable dread, named *Kenaima*. I met plenty of people, from a self-confident woman graduate in Trinidad, to a less certain mineralogist who had lived half his life among Indians, who were willing to explain *Kenaima* to me and each told me something different. All the books on the country mention *Kenaima*, many at some length. Its existence and importance cannot be doubted; baptism and even continual contact with Europeans do little to dispel its terror; it is as deep-rooted in the belief of the clothed, English-speaking Indians who work timber at Batika and Mazaruni as of the unsophisticated people in the Pakaraima Mountains, but no one has yet discovered what exactly constitutes it. All unexplained deaths are attributed to *Kenaima*, certain places are to be avoided on account of *Kenaima*, strangers may be *Kenaimas*, people can set a *Kenaima* on you, you are in danger of *Kenaima* if you associate with men of another tribe. Various ceremonial acts are necessary to propitiate *Kenaima*. It is certainly something malevolent and super-natural, that is all that can be said certainly of it.

It is as well to be highly sceptical of all statements made about primitive beliefs, particularly at the present moment when so much information is being confidently doled out to the public at third hand in the innumerable popular 'Outlines' of culture. These are usually *précis*, with the qualifications omitted, of weightier books which for the most part are collections of untravelled scholars; the authority ultimately depends on evidence of explorers and travellers, and only those who have some acquaintance with the difficulties of obtaining this evidence know what sort of value to attribute to it. At least two-thirds of it is derived from interrogations conducted either through interpreters (the most unsatisfactory form of conver-sation even on the simplest matters) or with an incomplete knowl-edge of the language. In any case the languages do not as a rule possess a vocabulary or syntax capable of accuracy, being devoid of abstract terms. And even were it possible for the primitive man to express what he believed – it is hard enough for the highly educated – he is invariably reluctant to do so. Even in the practical questions of direction – as appeared when I asked the Indian at Takutu ford whether I had reached the Sauriwau creek – his natural inclination is to tell the inquirer what he thinks he wishes to hear. This is still more the case in dealing with intimate and embarrassing questions about his private beliefs.

I encountered a very clear instance of this fallability of opinion in the case of *Kenaima*. Two Europeans, who had exceptional opportunities of studying Indians, had earned their confidence and had certainly devoted most of their life to them, gave me completely contradictory explanations of the belief. One said that it was the power of evil, the abstract malevolent and destructive principle in life, working for its own end, sometimes in concrete form either human or animal, in order to injure and kill; the other that it was the art by which a human enemy was able to develop supernatural advantages, become a beast, like the leopard men, werewolves, etc., of universal reputation, travel immense distances instantaneously, go without food, become invisible and so on, in order to accomplish his revenge. I can imagine either of these statements finding its way into a textbook and becoming part of the material for anthropological hypothesis. Both cannot be wholly true and probably neither is. Possibly *Kenaima* is supernatural evil, always present and active, which can on occasions be canalized by magic and used for a human motive, in which case the revenger is possessed by evil to such an extent that for the time being he is *Kenaima*. That is merely a guess. I quote the two confidently definite explanations as being noticeable contributions to the general scepticism that is one of the more valuable fruits of travel.

Another rather more arduous march left us still depressingly close to the point of our departure; as on the day before, we scrambled up and down, through bush where the trail was almost lost and had to be cleared step by step with cutlasses, turning on our tracks and wading through creeks – one of them the Echilifar, deep and very fast, so that it was hard to keep our feet. As before, whenever we attempted to rest, we were beset with cabouris. At half-past eleven we reached a hut inhabited by a Negress who had been brought up by one of the servants of the Boundary Commission and left there. She gave us fresh milk and four addled eggs. We put up our hammocks in her house and the shade and swaddlings of handkerchiefs and towels gave us some respite from fly. After an hour and a half we resumed the march; at half-past four Antonio gave a loud holla, which was taken up by the following men, and we came in sight of a village of three huts, apparently nameless; there was a fourth partially ruinous hut which we were offered for our camp and unwisely accepted; unwisely because the place was alive with fleas, *djiggas* and ticks.

We seemed popular here for the people greeted us with unusual cordiality, and besides the ceremonial bowl of *cassiri* laid out for us on the ground a great dish of cassava bread (not unlike oat cake) and earthenware bowls of peppers and stewed leaf (not unlike spinach). I was intensely thirsty and, seeing Father Keary drink some of the *cassiri*, did so too. It was agreeable and enormously refreshing, so that always after this, when it was offered, I drank a pint or more with increasing appreciation.

Attempting to check our position on the map by inquiries from Antonio, I found that we were even nearer Tipuru than I had thought, for the two mountains Yewaile and Tawaling, marked several miles apart, are, according to Antonio, two humps on the same spur of hill, and our whole afternoon's march had been merely to encircle this. Father Keary did not share the geographical interests of the early missionaries of his Society and was wholly oblivious to his position or direction. It was his habit to spend most of the day's march telling his beads, quietly following Antonio from one sphere of his true activity to the next. Before supper that evening he baptized a child and married the parents.

We were able to purchase two cocks here with Woolworth bracelets, one of which we killed for supper and the other carried on alive for the next day. It is a curious fact that though most Indian households keep a few fowls they do not use them or their eggs for food; indeed the birds, which live frugally on what they can pick up round the houses, are barely eatable. They are kept because the Indians find the crowing of the cocks at night a comforting sound, likely to scare away *Kenaimas*, and also as measure of time, for they crow pretty regularly at an hour's interval from midnight until dawn.

The night was one of exceptional discomfort, for the moonlight streamed through the ruined roof of the hut, brightly illuminating the interior, with the result that the cabouris kept awake; there were also mosquitoes in fair numbers (I was not using my net at the time and did not wish to disturb the boys to find it among the baggage) and they, with the fleas already mentioned, made sleep difficult; the *djiggas* and ticks were also at work but did not cause immediate pain. All that was needed to complete the discomfort of night was rain, and this began in a steady downpour some hours before dawn, just when the setting of the moon offered some relief from the cabouris. The boys crowded into the hut but were little better off, for there was no roof of any consequence; so we lit a small fire and sat scratching and shivering until daylight. Father Keary said Mass in the smoky gloom of one of the houses, and we set out again in the rain, scarcely at all refreshed by our night's rest.

That day's march was three long and steep climbs, with two small descents, one to cross the Yowiparu creek, and the other to a bush valley beside the Kowa river where we made camp. We stopped to eat some bananas at the summit of one of the hills but were too tired to trouble about having a meal prepared before supper; then we killed our own cock and ate it in the inevitable swarm of cabouris. But the bush where we camped was tall and dense so that the moonlight did not penetrate to us; the flies disappeared at sunset and we got ten hours' undisturbed sleep.

Next day, for the first time, we seemed to make real progress; the line lay more or less straight, mounting all the way, mostly through open country. We left camp at 6.45 and, taking an hour and a half's rest between 11 and 12.30, reached Karto, the first of the Patamona villages, at 4.45. The last few hours were very painful, first climbing a hillside of sharp pebbles in the full glare of the afternoon sun, and then crossing a dead flat tableland of hot, iron-hard earth.

There were three houses at Karto and an open shelter where we slept. The people were cheerful and hospitable, bringing out, as before, *cassiri*, peppers, cassava bread and vegetable. Here, for the first time, we met women wearing no clothes except their little bead aprons. There were no cabouris or mosquitoes here, but there was little sleep, for the old bites were continuously at work; we were at a considerable height and it was bitterly cold after sundown; also the *djiggas*, inflamed by the day's walk, began to make themselves felt.

These are small insects which live in and round houses; they work their way through one's boots to the soles of one's feet where they drill holes and lay their eggs, preferably under the toenails or any hard piece of skin; the process is painless or at least unnoticeable among the numerous other bites that torment one. In a day the eggs have begun to grow; they continue to do so at great rapidity, raising a lump which is at first irritating and later painful. If allowed to remain they hatch out into maggots in the foot and serious poisoning sets in. Their removal is a perfectly simple process if performed by someone native to the place; the eggs are in a little, onion-shaped envelope and it is essential that this shell be removed unbroken, otherwise an egg remains and hatches out. People who live in places liable to *djiggas* usually have their feet examined by their servant every evening after their bath. He opens up the hole with a pin and dexterously picks out the bag of eggs intact. I had seen Antonio and his wife attending each other in this way several times during the journey. I felt two or three *djiggas* during the night and asked Antonio to get them out next morning. When he came to do so he found a dozen more and got them all out without difficulty; the operation was practically painless.

It had painful consequences, however, for when I came to walk I found that what with the bruising of the day before and the several small punctures, I was exceedingly lame in both feet. Fortunately we had not far to go and with the help of numerous swigs of brandy, and two sticks, I was able to hobble along at about half the usual pace and four times the usual effort, and just made Kurikabaru, the next village, before giving out, feeling that I had in some measure atoned for whatever suffering I had inflicted on the town clerk's horse on the journey from Boa Vista.

We spent two nights at Kurikabaru; a little hut was at our disposal, built of bark and divided into four minute cubicles, dark and draughty. I spent most of the time there, lying in my hammock. It was a bleak village, thirteen huts scattered on a desolate hill top, and the people were impoverished and dour. There was rain some of the time and a continuous, raw wind; the height by the aneroid was a little under three thousand feet; I slept with shirt, trousers, and stockings over my pyjamas, but even then was cold at night under the blanket. There was dust and refuse blowing about all day when the rain did not keep it down. The people kept to their houses, huddled in the woodsmoke. The Macushi droghers were ill at ease

136

there and my three wished to go home; loads had grown lighter – in fact we were now uncomfortably short of provisions – and they could easily be spared. Eusebio stayed on and I engaged a Patamona man to carry what was left of my things.

Paying the droghers was a complicated process as it had to be done in powder packed in little red flasks, shot, gun-caps and necklaces; in the end I had not enough to go round, for I had been frivolously open-handed at the beginning of the journey, making presents to anyone with an amiable manner. The droghers had to take dollar notes for some of their wages; they accepted them with the apparent lassitude they maintained in all their dealings and tucked them away in their loin cloths, from which *cache*, if they had not disintegrated, as seemed probable, during the journey, they would no doubt pass from hand to hand from the hills to the savannah until eventually they reached Mr Figuiredo.

I also sent a messenger ahead to find Mr Winter with a note warning him of our approach and throwing myself on his kindness for provisions and transport down the Potaro.

Provisions were running short. When I had given the droghers rations for their return journey, we were left without meat and barely enough *farine* to last the boys four days. Of the personal stores of Father Keary and myself, there was a fair amount of coffee, some rapidly coagulating sugar, two cupfuls of rice, one-eighth of a bottle of brandy, a tin of sardines and a tin of salmon. There was nothing to be got in Kurikabaru except a few bananas. In these circumstances it was impossible to stay on there so we set out again on the second day. On the last evening a hunter came in with a small deer, of which we were able to secure a leg.

It was hunger rather than restored fitness that decided us on the march. The holes from the *djiggas* were now mostly healed over, but I was suffering from an inflamed toe where one of them had become slightly poisoned. It was astonishing and slightly ludicrous that so small a disability could effect one so much – a single minute limb, shiny, rosy and increased by half of an inch at the most in girth, made one dead lame; walking was acutely unpleasant; not only was every step very painful but the effort to the rest of the body was absurdly magnified, so that an hour's march exhausted one as much as four hours of normal progress. It was annoying too for the rest of the expedition who were obliged to adapt their pace to my limp, for it is every bit as distressing to be held back on a march as to be pushed on.

Fortunately the next stage was a very short one, and by cutting the side out of my boot to ease the swelling, I was able to make it in four hours. We left the open hills now and entered the forest which stretches from there, unbroken, to the coast; there were no more invigorating changes of view, prospects of river and mountain suddenly disclosed and as suddenly shut out as though the curtain had fallen on the act of a play; no shifting of horizon, five miles distant at dawn, fifty miles distant at noon; no confidence, no possibility of surprise, that urged one up the steepest and most fiery hillside with eagerness to see what was beyond; instead there was a twilit green tunnel, leaves on each side and overhead, leaves in front that had to be cut clear as we advanced and, underfoot, slippery leaf-mould or a cruel network of bare roots.

We were still crossing Amazon waters; the creeks we crossed and recrossed were tributaries of the Tumong, which in its turn ran into the Ireng, and so by the Rio Branco past Boa Vista into the Rio Negro, the Amazon, and the South Atlantic. During the next two days we passed the continental divide where the waters start flowing towards the Caribbean, feeding the Potaro and Essequibo, but there was no clearly defined watershed; the streams dovetailed into one another, the source of the Kowa, which is Amazon water, being north of the source of the Murabang which runs eventually to the Essequibo; the official map of this river system was wildly inaccurate, and what with my complaints about the complexity of the geography, and my lameness, I must, I think, have proved a very tiresome travelling companion to Father Keary.

There was nothing to give beauty or excitement to that morning's journey, except a fine waterfall which we came to unexpectedly; a sunless pool, over-arched with branches into which a stream fell sheer, twenty or thirty feet, but no rainbows shone round it and the spray rose dull as sea mist, to meet the falling water.

Our camp that afternoon was the least attractive we had yet made. We came on an acre of cleared ground surrounded on all sides by bush. There had once been a village there in the days of Father Carey-Elwes, and since it had no name when he discovered it, he christened the place Santa Maria. Now there was only one house and the desolation was accentuated by the tattered ruin of a shelter erected two years back by the Boundary Commissioners, and now reduced to a half-capsized skeleton of beams and rafters, and a few shreds of waterproof cardboard hanging forlornly from what had been the roof. There was no flowing water here; instead a patch of marsh which deepened towards the centre into a shallow and opaque pool. We camped in the bush near it, slinging our hammocks among a variety of biting and stinging flies and a million or so ants, which rapidly invaded our provisions until we hung them too from the trees.

The space round the house was unswept, littered with bones and rags and broken earthenware; the people remarkable in their poverty and unkempt condition even among their race. The younger members were little used to visitors and hid indoors, crowding about the sides of the door, sometimes emerging and then darting back with silly giggling. The older ones attempted to show some hospitality but the *cassiri* they brought out was warm and only half-fermented.

I had expected to find my messenger here with a reply from Mr Winter, but there was no sign of him. The people reported that he had passed through two days before, but he had his bow and arrows with him and they supposed he had seen game. Nothing will deflect an Indian from following food. I had heard that often a whole boat's crew would desert if they saw a herd of bush pig, and follow it for days, returning after an orgy of meat-eating to their employers and quite uncomprehending the vexation they might have aroused.

The people at Santa Maria did not know exactly where Mr Winter was. He was within two days' journey, they said, but he had left his home at Anundabaru some years ago.

In all these depressing circumstances there was one hopeful feature – a fat little stallion trailing his halter, at grass near the house. The Indians were not only willing to hire him out, but would accept a dollar note in payment. This solved the only pressing problem which was how, in my crippled condition, I was going to get to Mr Winter's before supplies gave out. There was, of course, no saddle or bridle, so I set out next morning soon after sunrise, a relieved, if highly comic, figure riding bare-back with Antonio leading the horse by his rope.

The bush line led up the Tumong, sometimes along the bank, sometimes meandering away from it, three times crossing it and finally, in contravention of everything the map suggested, leaving it on our left. There were also numerous smaller streams to cross, all running through precipitous little glens. It was possible to ride, for about half the way, on the alternate half-miles that lay along the tops of the ridges; climbs in and out of the valley had to be done on foot, the stallion being left to find his own perilous way through them, from rock to rock, over fallen or under half-reclining tree trunks, but always emerging steaming and patient on the opposing summit. The riding was far from pleasurable, for the line was, in its best places, but head-high for foot passengers and the breadth of a single file and, in its worst, totally obscured, so that to the normal discomfort of bare vertebrae was added constant scratching and whipping across the face and buffeting of the legs against tree trunks which, on the injured side, were agonizing. It provided, however, the necessary stimulus of expectancy, for while I was riding – face down, blind on the horse's neck and nervously anticipating more jostling than ever came to the swollen foot – I longed avidly to walk; and while I walked – hobbling one pace to every two up and down the sides of the valleys – I longed to ride; and as the intervals between changes were of short duration, there were frequently recurring moments of delight when I first found myself astride the sharp ridge and sweaty sides of the horse, and first on my foot again, when it became necessary to dismount. In this way, after an hour's rest between eleven and twelve, we reached our destination before four o'clock.

On the way we met my returning messenger who had had no sport on his journey but had taken three nights instead of one for the sake of his own ease. He brought a large key and, attached to it, a note from Mr Winter which read: *Delighted you are coming. You will find me half a day's good walking from Anundabaru. Your boy seems to have taken a long time coming which was unfortunate as I sent my boat down to Kangaruma for mail at six this morning. If he had arrived earlier I would have held it back. However, no doubt it will return and in the fullness of Patamona time can go down again. Of course stay here with me till then. You have come at a bad time as I am extremely short of provisions. Here is the key of Anundabaru House where you can camp on the way, but it is probably in bad repair.*

Earlier in the year I might have regarded this as a major misfortune, but I was by now so well used to the checks and annoyances of travelling that I was unable to blame the messenger very heartily. After all it would have been an unnatural coincidence if I *had* caught the boat and, as it turned out, there was a rough fifteen miles walk between Mr Winter's camp and the river, which I would have been in no condition to undertake at that moment.

For nearly a mile square round Anundabaru the trees were all down, having been demolished by a government botanist who wished to test a theory that a tropical rain forest would not burn. By good fortune the house escaped the conflagration. The earth was still black with wood ash but bracken had grown up to a height of six or ten feet. A wood shack stood in the centre near the Anundabura creek. It was a modest building but seemed spacious after the huts where we had slept lately, and, since it was the first building of sawn wood since Hart's, remarkably civilized. It was built on piles, with three rooms and a little verandah. An Indian, settled near it, had utilized the lower storey as a store and shelter for live stock.

We climbed the somewhat rickety steps and as we were supervising the arrangement of baggage, Antonio pointed out that our trouser legs were covered with fleas. So were all our clothes, and a closer scrutiny revealed that the earth between the bracken and the house was covered with them, as densely as though by ants; enormous creatures, twice the usual size, hopping everywhere in the dust. But their bulk was their undoing, for we were able to pick them off before they had done much biting.

That night at supper Father Keary and I finished the last of our provisions, keeping only a few bananas for next morning's breakfast. We went to our hammocks as usual at sunset and were peacefully asleep when at about nine, rain began. It was then clear what Mr Winter meant when he warned us that the house might be in bad repair. It happened that I had the worse room, and I awoke to find water pouring in on me and to hear it on all sides. It was absolutely dark and the matches on the floor by my side were already sodden and useless. I began a difficult investigation, treading carefully round the floor in the hope of finding a dry patch. Presently I heard Father Keary awake, striking matches in his room. We lit a scrap of ballata that we found lying about, and by its light were able to see the extent of our discomfort. There was a long dry strip in Father Keary's room where he could hang his hammock. We assembled the more perishable luggage – photographic films, notebooks, matches, etc. – under this. My room was completely swamped except for one corner, about a yard square. Here the ballata gave out, but by striking matches we were able to hang the hammock in a U, with the centre, when it was weighted down, just clear of the floor. Here I sat with my head on my knees until dawn, damp, sleepless and uncharitably intolerant of the stertorous snores which rose above the splash of the water from Father Keary's room next door.

It was still raining pitilessly at dawn next morning. I went down to see how the boys had fared, who had camped in the Indian's hut. They too were wet and depressed, huddled round the fire in an atmosphere thick with smoke and steam, reeking of men, animals and wet thatch.

The little creek by the house had swollen overnight into a broad, swift torrent of brown water, full of mud and leaves and dead wood. There were a number of larger creeks between there and Mr Winter's and a brief consultation with Antonio convinced me that they and the slippery state of the ground made it impossible to take the stallion any further. Accordingly, so as not to hold up the expedition, I set out first with one man as guide, expecting to be caught up by the others before I reached Mr Winter's. As it turned out, however, I got there a few minutes before them, for the cold water through which we were constantly passing eased my foot and the rough nature of the line made the journey more of an obstacle race than a walk – a matter of scrambling over tree trunks and rocks, using hands as much as feet; this nearly equalized our chances.

I had met Mr Winter on a convivial evening at Christmastime in the Georgetown hotel, and he now greeted me as an old friend. He was equally genial to Father Keary, offering him every facility if he wished to include the camp, where a considerable village had grown up, in his annual itinerary. But with practical clarity he explained his present position. He was down to the last bin in all provisions and could do nothing towards rationing the boys. He could put me up until I found a means of getting downriver; he could give Father Keary a fowl and some eggs for his own use, but he had no *farine*, dried meat or rice to spare. In the circumstances Father Keary had to make an immediate retreat to Kurikabaru which, without the handicap of my lameness, could be done comfortably in two days. There he would probably be able to collect cassava and yams. It was not a very satisfactory prospect and I watched him go with concern – but there was no possible alternative.

About one concomitant arrangement I felt some personal guilt. Eusebio had to go back too. The unfortunate youth had endured all the discomforts of the march – and he made it abundantly plain that he took them as great discomforts – in the hope of visiting Georgetown, and now that all the stiffest walking was over, and there remained, for the most part, only a leisurely river journey, well suited to his disposition, he found himself headed back, all the way he had come, through the hills again, down to the savannah and his native village. I paid him a large compensation, but both of us knew that the other knew that no compensation could really suffice. I am still ashamed at his betrayal, but, again, there was no alternative. Not only was Mr Winter unable to feed him, but he expressly refused to have a Macushi in his camp, upsetting his Patamona workmen. The labour supply was precarious and at any untoward happening the Indians were liable to melt away silently to their villages.

As he unpacked for me, Eusebio's face betrayed that reproach, wistfulness and melancholy that only plump and rather ignoble faces can adequately express.

Poor Eusebio! I am sure Georgetown would have the worst possible effect on him, but I hope he gets there some time, in some fashion, and does not for ever nurture resentment for my breach of faith.

EIGHT

Diamond washing and selling – Upper Potaro – a bad family – Kaieteur – Lower Potaro – Amatuk

We had descended constantly from Kurikabaru but Winter's camp stood at a considerable height; high enough to be cool most of the day and cold between midnight and dawn. There was usually a mist for the first three or four hours of day, which gradually lifted, revealing the great bulk of Mount Kowatipu, five or six miles away across the valley. This was a long, flat-topped spur, with sharply precipitous, bush-clad cliffs. There was said to be a lake on its summit, but no white man has ever been there and no Indian has first-hand knowledge of it.

The camp was built on a cleared hilltop between the valleys of the Mikraparu creek and the Murabang river, which runs into the Kopinang, officially regarded as a tributary of the Potaro, but according to Winter, who is one of the few men who have visited it, the real river, carrying a far greater volume of water than the stream marked on the maps as the upper Potaro. It was the Mikraparu creek which Winter was working for alluvial diamonds.

The camp consisted of a bark store-house, a little hut with thatched roof and stake walls which we used as a dining-room and a larger house under construction where we slept; this room had a floor and walls made of bark and a roof of waterproof paper. It was entirely constructed by a Patamona Indian named Thomas who had recently left his wife on account of her having given birth to twins – certain evidence of infidelity to an Indian mind. Winter had been there two or three years and already had a lime and a pau-pau tree bearing well; there were also a large number of hens whose eggs formed an important part of our diet. As he had warned me, provisions were low, particularly flour, rice and sugar. We began in great luxury with bacon, tinned butter, tinned milk and toast, but after a week were reduced to yams and eggs and whatever the hunters brought in.

Winter kept two hunters in his employment who were paid by results. Sometimes they would bring in two or three bush cows in a week, he said, and then there would be meat rations for the whole camp. While I was there they were unlucky, often bringing nothing at all; occasionally, however, they would kill an excellent bird called *mahm*, not unlike a pheasant in size and flavour, or a water rodent called *labba*, that tasted like pork. Bush turkey and bush pig, the other most abundant game, were flesh of no particular flavour or quality.

Winter had never tasted *cassiri* and was sceptical of my praise of it. However, he had some made and the two women who looked after the house knew a method of fermenting it which did not involve spitting. He agreed with me that it was excellent. We also unearthed in his store a keg of crude spirit that had been sent originally for making embrocation; with brown sugar and limes it made a fiery aperitif which we used to drink at sundown after our baths.

Scattered at some distance from the house were the huts inhabited by the fluctuating body of Indian workers. It was a year-old experiment to employ Indians, which so far was giving excellent results. Negroes had to be transported to and from the coast and paid comparatively high wages on their journey; while at work they expected rations of meat, dried fish, sugar, rice, and flour. The Indians drifted into camp with wives and children, worked for a month or two until they had acquired the object they coveted, usually a gun, and then drifted back to their homes. While they were there they lived simply, happy enough as long as they had plenty of *farine* and yams and an occasional orgy of meat, and their wives and older children joined in the work. It seemed an idyllic arrangement. They were thriftless with their possessions and easily broke them or exchanged them for something of far lower value which happened to take their fancy, and so would return eventually to do another spell of work. Winter was extraordinarily clever in coaxing labour out of the villagers.

Whenever he went to Georgetown he came back with some new supply of novelties, knowing that once these began circulating in the villages and it became known that they were obtainable at his store, he would begin tapping sources he could never reach himself. He had a great success shortly after Christmas with some mechanical mice, emerald green drawers and a gramophone. When I first arrived my hat and red blanket excited great cupidity, everyone asking Winter how long he would have to work to earn one like them and why he had never seen them in the store. There was a kindergarten atmosphere about the camp; the little wives would often stop in their work to play. Any at all painful accident, such as a boy falling from a ladder and breaking his rib, was greeted with an outburst of wild merriment.

These Indians were mostly from the Kopinang banks and had never seen missionaries, policemen or white men of any kind before. They arrived naked and went away heavily swathed in calico; a few even took hats and high-heeled shoes, but I got the impression that they were attracted by them as toys rather than finery and that when they got home they would be put away and played with, not flaunted before their less travelled neighbours. It was astonishing to see how easily these very simple people adapted themselves to the mechanism of the trommel but they worked without system, as though it were all part of a game; when shovelling earth they would throw one spadeful high and the next low, sometimes several in quick succession, sometimes a few very slowly. I never saw less coercion in any country in the world. Had any been attempted, there would have been no complaints or protests; the Indians would simply have left the wages due to them, packed up and gone away, as they have often treated impatient travellers in the past. They have by nature and upbringing no sense of authority. In most languages the first word one learns is 'sir'; few of the Indian languages – I think none – have any term of subservience or respect. The chiefs of the villages have no power and no privileges. They are elected for any sort of eminence – in one case because the man was cited as witness in a police case and came back from Annai with such prestige that the former chief was instantly deposed – and exercise no judicial function. Nor are they supported by contributions from the village. You do not in Indian villages find those luxurious old men, common enough in Africa, squatting at ease among a dozen wives and sniffing an ammonia bottle while their huts are piled up with yams and manioc by their subjects. Every now and then a black 'pork knocker' will work his way up into Indian country and attempt to assert himself in a village, taking up with the women and bullying the men. The Indians are afraid of the blacks on account of their size and strength and for a little will do what they are told. Then they lose patience and one of two things happens; either they all decamp silently and leave him to starve or he is stealthily murdered, poisoned or shot full of arrows in the back. Several black adventurers have come to a bad end in this way, but that has been mostly in Macushi country. The Kopinang people have lived unmolested.

While I was at Winter's, however, a report came in of a party of 'pork knockers' who were working down the Yawong on the other side of Mount Kowatipu; they had conscripted the Indians whom Winter had sent for from Baramakatoi to cut lines round his concession and were using them as droghers. They were said to be making for Brazil.

The law against black immigration into the native reserves can, of course, rarely be enforced. No policeman or officer of the Government had ever passed through the country where I now was. The nearest policeman was at Bartika, ten days' journey away and the nearest magistrate at Bon Success. It was, in fact, an extremely lonely camp, with no neighbours at all. The nearest white man was at Mazaruni station, a few miles from the coast. There was no through traffic; I was the first guest Winter had entertained since his settlement there. Moreover, it is getting more lonely. Ten years before there had been East Indian and Portuguese stores all down the Potaro between Kaieteur and Kangaruma. Now there are none at all. There had also been a German planter at the mouth of the Chinapowu whose estate was largely marked on the map, but, as I was to find later, there was no trace of it except some bamboos and fruit trees, smothered and reverting to wilder forms in the bush.

I spent ten days waiting for Winter's boat to return, during which my foot slowly mended. After a week the nail came off and I was perfectly well; until then I kept to my hammock most of the day.

Winter was a delightful host and companion; middle-aged, genial, cynical, personally optimistic. Race – pure white Creole; education – technical, engineering and surveying, mostly in the United States and Canada; married, with wife and family in Barbados whom he visited whenever he could; religion – Anglo-Israelite; politics – socialist turned conservative on finding himself a capitalist and employer of labour; general contempt and suspicion of all officials; generous, businesslike, witty; personally optimistic for he always examined his sieve with the expectation of finding the large stone that was going to make his fortune.

As my foot got better I often went down with him to the workings. He was washing for alluvial gold and diamonds in the bed of the Mikraparu, and to do this had dammed and canalized the little creek. The dam was made of timber and mud, held together with ropes of bush vine and attached to the surrounding trees, and the piping that conducted the water to the trommel was of hollowed wood. With the exception of a small hand-pump, worked by a deaf and dumb girl, the entire mechanism had been constructed on the spot. It had the appearance of a drawing by Mr Heath Robinson, but it seemed to work. The trommel was a horizontal cylindrical sieve made of wire gauze of varying mesh; it was rotated by hand, two girls spinning it with wooden handles. The gravel from the bed of the stream was brought up in barrows and emptied into the trommel where it was washed down by the water from the stream. As it went down all the heavier and smaller stones fell through into a tray. At the end of the sieve only large pebbles emerged and were shovelled into a heap by two more girls. The hard work of digging out the gravel and wheeling it up to the trommel was done by their men.

The gold dust, being the heaviest constituent of the mud in the tray, went to the bottom and passed through a mercury trap where it was collected; any larger nuggets remained with the mud, in which would also be the diamonds, and were washed down into another fine sieve called a jig. This was gently swayed up and down in a tank of water until all the soluble matter had disappeared. The product was a sieve full of very fine gravel containing whatever diamonds and gold nuggets had been in the load. The whole process was exceedingly simple. I never knew if the Indians had any clear idea of the purpose of the various tasks set them; they performed them in the half-listless, half-frivolous manner I have indicated. A black foreman named Gerry worked at the digging with the men and generally kept operations in motion in Winter's absence. His main job was to get the Indians out of their hammocks in the morning and to blow a whistle for them to stop at the end of the day.

The only skilled labour was Winter's, in searching the jig; it was full of beryls, clear white stones which, when wet and glistening, seemed to me indistinguishable from the diamonds. These, on the days I went, were invariably minute and singularly unimpressive. A good day's yield was six or seven carats in twenty-five stones, most of them tarnished and opaque, and two or three fragments of gold the size of rice grains. These were all put carefully into a cartridge case, weighed and sealed up. (The diamonds were cleaned up with hydrofluoric acid and boiled in *aqua regia* before they reached the market.) I never acquired any skill in picking them out, though the usual maxim is that though it is possible to mistake another stone for a diamond, it is impossible ever to mistake a diamond for anything else. It is said to have a metallic sheen that belongs to no other stone, but I always needed to have it shown to me before I recognized it.

The diamond trade of Guiana is on a far smaller scale and organized in a more haphazard fashion than in the great diamond fields of South Africa. There are no large corporations controlling the output; no smuggling and illicit diamond buying. The workers are all solitary prospectors or handfuls of friends trying their luck in common. Very few of them have any knowledge of geology; they work up the rivers and creeks until their rations are exhausted or until they have made a strike good enough to warrant their return to the coast. They then celebrate their good fortune in a few months' high living and either look for other work or drift back again to the bush in the hope of another success. No fortunes have ever been made there. The market is in the hands of Jews and Portuguese in Georgetown, most of whom have agents buying for them up-river. If an agent is thought by his employers to have paid too much for a stone, he is liable to have it returned to him and the price stopped out of his wages. Some sellers make a habit of going from one jeweller to another with their diamonds in the hope of finding a higher offer. They are completely in the hands of the buyers because few of them understand the subtleties of colouring that determine the value of a stone. But they gain little by their negotiations, for a buyer does not like to take a stone after he has once made an offer, for it means that his bid has been the highest and that he is paying more than his rival's valuation.

There are certain stones of known defects that have been changing hands in the colony for years. As soon as any newcomer appears in the market they are all offered to him. One in particular is famous; a twenty-four carat stone of negligible value on account of flaws and discoloration. The original discoverer boiled it in *aqua regia* and produced on it a series of minute surface cracks which gave it a dull, whitish appearance that on casual inspection might belong to a good stone in rough condition. A buyer paid $100 a carat for it as a gamble (the normal value would be $210) and had it returned to him by the merchants at headquarters. However, he was able to sell it again before the story got round, and since then it has been bought and resold four or five times, the last holder being faced with a dead loss until some stranger appears to take it off him. It is like the knave of clubs in the nursery game of 'Black Sambo'.

Winter had innumerable stories of the country, which he used to recount with superb pungency over supper, and as we sat in our hammocks in the evening. There was one of a cook of his who had come to him highly qualified, a fugitive from her home. She had been taken by a missionary at an early age and taught the domestic arts and virtues in a Georgetown college. At adolescence she became haunted by the claustrophobia that affects all Indians when they come to town, and, urged by her instinct, made for her native bush. But she was by now neither civilized nor primitive. She arrived after long absence at her mother's house, armed with her certificate for proficiency on the pianoforte, umbrella in hand, sun bonnet on her head. She found a strange, naked woman who was her mother, eagerly welcoming her to a one-roomed hut, full of wood smoke and poultry. More than this, she found a naked young man who had been selected by her mother as a husband. Numerous suitors appeared, attracted by the glamour of her urban education, but all equally savage, uncouth and unacceptable. A common enough situation in countries where educational experiments are practised, but in this case distinguished by a less usual conclusion. The original suitor, at last losing patience with her superiority and aloofness, married the mother and the two proceeded to make the hut still less habitable for her. So she packed up her umbrella and bonnet and musical diploma, and enjoyed a brief elopement with a passing catechist. After which she became Mr Winter's cook, and so excellently had she been taught at her coast school that he was at the moment making strenuous efforts to retrieve her from the holiday she was taking among the Negro boating community downriver.

But most of Winter's stories depended for their point on his belief in the incompetence and dishonesty of all government officials, and so cannot suitably be transcribed here. Moreover, they need the surroundings in which they were told, the lamplight in the half-finished shed, the surrounding camp-fires of the Indian huts and, beyond them, invisible in the dark but sensible, the forest and the dominant cliffs of Kowatipu.

Much of this chronicle – perhaps, it may seem, too much – has dealt with the difficulties of getting from place to place. But that seems to me unavoidable, for it is the preoccupation of two-thirds of the traveller's waking hours and the matter of all his nightmares. It is by crawling on the face of it that one learns a country; by the problems of transport that its geography becomes a reality and its inhabitants real people. Were one to be levitated on a magic carpet and whisked overnight from place to place, one would see all that was remarkable but it would be a very superficial acquaintance, and, in the same way, if one leaves the reader out of one's confidence – disavowing all the uncertainties of the route, the negotiations, projects and frustrations, making of oneself one of those rare, exemplary dragomans who disguise every trace of effort and present themselves before their employers with a plan completely tabulated, hampers packed, conveyances assembled, servants in attendance – one may show them some pretty spectacles and relate some instructive anecdotes, but one will not have given them what was originally offered when one was engaged, a share in the experience of travel, for these checks and hesitations constitute the genuine flavour.

I feel this strongly about those who travel in aeroplanes. They take with them, wherever they go, from start to finish, a single series of problems involving fuel, mechanism and air conditions. The features of geography and the character of the people are involved incidentally and indirectly. If one travels in the manner of the country, taking horses or cars where possible, walking when necessary, getting rations and labour where one can, using regular services of transport when one comes across them and fitting out expeditions of one's own where no facilities exist, one identifies oneself with the place one is visiting in a way that is impossible to the perhaps more courageous fliers. That, anyhow, is how I was travelling. There had hitherto been two main phases of the journey: by horse in the cattle country and by foot in the hills. Now I was to start on another, by boat down the rivers.

The situation was this: all regular service for mail and the delivery of stores, upstream from the coast, stopped at a depot named Kangaruma on the lower Potaro. It was there that Winter's stores were awaiting him. Between Kangaruma and the mouth of the Chinapowu – a day's march from his camp and the highest navigable point of the river – there were three obstacles, Amatuk falls, Waratuk falls and the Kaieteur. It was possible, by unloading it and carefully paying it out on a rope, to get a boat over Waratuk. Amatuk and, of course, Kaieteur were impossible. Thus, in getting down three separate boats were needed, one from Chinapowu to Kaieteur, another from Kaieteur to Amatuk, a third from Amatuk to Kangaruma. In getting stores upstream droghers were needed to carry them from landing to landing; in the case of Kaieteur this was a formidable process, as there was a two-mile portage, half of which was a sharp precipice. The river above Amatuk is uninhabited so that the labour had to be sent down and brought back with the stores. It was again needed to carry them from Chinapowu to the camp up a fifteen-mile trail, part of which was also precipitous. Thus 'sending down for stores' was not so simple a process as the words suggest. There was a further difficulty – that Winter owned only two of the three boats needed; between Amatuk and Kangaruma the only boat belonged to a Portuguese, ominously named Diabolo; there was no reason to suppose that it would be at Amatuk when we arrived; moreover, its owner was in a position of absolute monopoly and able to exact any charge he liked for its use. Winter's Negro foreman spoke gloomily of Diabolo's ill-nature.

I mentioned in the last chapter that Winter had sent a man down to Kangaruma for mail. He now eagerly awaited his return so that the boats could be used to send down for stores. On the eighth day the man came, a black named Sobers, and on the tenth we started out. There was difficulty about collecting droghers; some passing Indians were recruited but two of them fell sick before starting so that in the end two men had to be taken away from the digging. Eventually the party consisted of these two, Sobers who was now being sent back to the coast for good, his usefulness being superseded by the Kopinang Indians, the black foreman Gerry, myself and a Patamona family consisting of father and mother, son aged eight or nine and a dog, which they insisted at the last minute in bringing with them; they were an unattractive trio, even apart from their dog. The woman was slatternly and ill-favoured even for one of her race, with gross bandy legs, filthy and ragged clothes; the males wore only the *lap*; they had hair like chows and furtive, unfriendly eyes. I engaged Sobers, a muscular ruffian with gold teeth, as my own servant; the Indians were under the orders of Gerry, and I was in the position of passenger in the boat.

The walk from Mikraparu to Chinapowu was through bush line and across creeks, little different from the way from Anundabaru except that there was one steep descent down which we slipped from tree trunk to tree trunk, and that I was no longer lame. I wondered how the droghers managed to get their burdens up that hillside on the return journey.

At Chinapowu there were a few remains of a Boundary Commission store house and some deserted Indian huts rapidly falling to ruin. Of the plantation house of Holmia no sign remained. The Clementis on their Roraima journey in 1916 recorded that it was then just visible in the encroaching bush. The cleared ground was now ten feet deep in a second growth, from which emerged in gross and rudimentary forms a few descendants of cereals and fruit trees. There was one building, deserted, but still more or less intact, which had been built as a trading station at the time when all that district was being worked for ballata; it was substantially built of sawn wood; inside there were still the shelves on which the stock had been displayed, a counter and a rusted weighing machine. The floor was filthy and crawling with *djiggas*, but I swept the counter clear and lay on that until, some time after the blacks and me, the Indians turned up with my hammock. I had divided the copy of *Martin Chuzzlewit*, giving Winter, who was out of all reading matter, the part I had read. I now enjoyed the last chapters until the light failed and it was necessary to try to sleep.

The boat was a small flat-bottomed craft just capable of carrying us all and the luggage. It was beached high above the level of the river; we got it emptied out and afloat soon after daybreak but were obliged to delay until half-past seven by the Indian family who insisted on making up the fire which they had kept smouldering under their hammocks all through the night and cooking themselves some maize cobs they had found in the bush – relics of Holmia. Kaieteur was a full day's journey and it was important to make it before nightfall, so that this delay aggravated the antipathy I had felt for them ever since I discovered their intention of travelling with a dog. (This sentiment may perhaps shock animal lovers, but let them remember that Indian pets are far more odious even than those of Europeans, and are the chief disseminators of fleas, ticks and *djiggas*.)

Our boat was not built for speed and, weighed deep as we were, made slow progress even with the help of the stream. The two blacks rowed with immense energy, taking a pleasure in their strength. They fitted up rowlocks, tied paddles to wooden poles and used them as oars. The two Indian boys paddled fairly consistently but the family sat in the stern with their dog, making little attempt to help. The man complained that he was sick, and when we handed paddles to the woman and boy they trailed them listlessly in the water for a little, then shipped them, and opened a clothful of putrid fish which they proceeded to munch for the greater part of the day. They were bush people unused to the river. I would gladly have left them behind, but they were needed as droghers for Winter's stores. Instead I attempted to set a good example by paddling myself and within half an hour regretted it bitterly. It has always seemed to me an unnatural form of propulsion in which one is pulling against one's own weight and exhausting half one's strength in forming a fulcrum. After an hour, I gave it up and the Patamonas went on placidly eating their revolting food, occasionally offering some particularly uneatable morsel to the dog.

The river banks were absolutely devoid of habitation: familiar walls of forest on either side. Sobers and Gerry exchanged reminiscences of various camping grounds (for it is a two- or three-day journey upstream from Kaieteur to Chinapowu) and of phenomenal conditions of flood or drought that they had known. The water was deep sepia in colour and absolutely smooth; every feature of the forest wall was duplicated there in minute detail – trunk and bush vine, tangled undergrowth, bare root and the blossoming cumulus of the summit – except when, occasionally, we reached a place where the surface was dappled with real petals, white, yellow and pink, floating past us, strewn profusely and irregularly from the treetops over a large area, single and in clusters, as though they were flowering in a meadow.

*

It was after five when we reached Kaieteur. The landing was, of course, some way above the falls and, leaving the boys to secure the boat and bring up the luggage, I hurried forward on foot to see them before it was dark. I had expected to be led there by the sound, but it was scarcely perceptible until one reached the brink, and even there so great was the depth that only a low monotone rose to greet one.

The path led across a rock plateau totally unlike the surrounding country, bare except for cactuses and a few flowers, scattered with quartz, pebbles and sponge-like growths of crystal. A faint path led to the edge of the precipice, and there a natural platform of rock allowed me to lie and study the extraordinary scene.

It has been described in detail by several travellers. I had arrived at the best time of day, for then, in late afternoon, the whole basin and gorge were clear of mist. The river was half-full. Some visitors have toiled up to find only a single spout of water over which they were able to stand astride. A Russian artist went there to paint it and was obliged to fill in the river from photographs and his imagination. That evening the whole centre of the lip was covered, and the water gently spilled over it as though from a tilted dish. At the edge it was brown as the river behind it, rapidly turning to white and half-way down dissolving in spray so that it hung like a curtain of white drapery. It fell sheer from its seven hundred-odd feet, for the cliff had been hollowed back in the centuries and the edge jutted over an immense black cavern. At the foot dense columns of spray rose to meet it so that the impression one received was that the water slowed down, hesitated and then began to reascend, as though a cinema film had been reversed. And not only reversed, but taken in slow motion, for just as aeroplanes, hurtling like bullets through the air, seem from the ground to be gently floating across the sky, so the height here delayed and softened the vast fall, like the mason's at Buckfast who, tumbling off the triforium, is said to have been caught half-way down by angels, lowered gently and set on his feet in the nave, breathless, bewildered but unhurt.

The basin below was heaped with rocks, reduced by distance to little boulders, among which the water was breaking in a high sea, wave after wave set in being by the fall, emanating outwards and smashing into spray against the banks like an incoming tide; half a dozen or so minor cataracts were visible down the gorge before the river regained its tranquillity.

But more remarkable, perhaps, than the fall itself was the scene in which it stood. The scale was immense, so that the margin of forest shrank to a line of shrub, and it was only by an effort that one could remind oneself that these were the great ramparts that had towered over us all day. The cleavage, too, was so abrupt that it appeared unnatural, as though two sections in a composite panorama had been wrongly fitted; above was the placid level on which we had travelled: below for miles ahead the river could be followed, shot black and silver ribbon, gently winding between bush-clad hills; and here, in the middle a sharp break where the edges, instead of coming together, lay apart, clumsily disjointed.

I lay on the overhanging ledge watching the light slowly fail, the colour deepen and disappear. The surrounding green was of density and intenseness that can neither be described nor reproduced: a quicksand of colour, of shivering surface and unplumbed depth, which absorbed the vision, sucking it down and submerging it. When it was quite dark I found my way back to the others.

There was a rest house in fair condition at the top of Kaieteur; this and the one at Amatuk had been erected at the time when a Georgetown company projected a regular tourist service, which had come to nothing. (A lady named Mrs McTurk carried on the goodwill of the concern and made the arrangements for anyone who wished to go up, but no caretaker or store was now kept at the falls.) There were numerous names and initials carved on the walls and Sobers said it was lucky to leave some trace of one's occupation. Gerry, however, was sceptical, saying, 'Most of dey is dead already.'

The most recent inscription was dated in January of that year and said, 'Alfredo Sacramento, Author and Globe Trotter starved here.'

I had heard this man's story from Winter. He was a Portuguese who appeared in Georgetown about Christmastime, with no claims to authorship but many to globetrotting. He was supporting himself by selling his own portrait on signed postcards. It is not a unique means of livelihood. I met a bearded Dane in Venice doing the same thing, and every now and then I see a brief interview in the English papers with someone who has successfully circumnavigated the

Earth in this way. Most of these travellers carry a recommendation, genuine or spurious, from some university professor, which, translated into six languages, proclaims their literary promise. Armed with this and a suitcase full of photographs of themselves in exploring costume, they set out to travel round the world. I do not know if any of them ever write books when they get home; their experience is mostly a monotonous round of café touting, incarceration and deportation, rows at consulates and immigration offices. (We gave the bearded Dane a list of addresses at which he should call when he came to England, but I have not yet heard of his arrival.)

Sacramento quickly exhausted the patience and curiosity of Georgetown and, taking up with some blacks in a rum shop, was told golden legends of the hospitality of the Indians and ranchers. Asking how he could get there, he was told that from Kaieteur there was a clear road through to Brazil, with Indian villages at every halt, where, though they were unlikely to buy his portrait, the people would feed him and help him on his way. The poor fellow believed all that he was told and began making inquiries about how he could reach Kaieteur. As it happened, there was in Georgetown at the time a Canadian doctor who, reading about Kaieteur in a magazine devoted to popular education, had impetuously taken a passage to Guiana and asked at the railway station for a ticket to the falls. Disgusted but undeterred by discovering the expedition to be more elaborate than he had expected, he was then arranging for a boat to take him up. The boat captains are always glad of an extra hand upstream, so Sacramento was able to get a free passage on condition of his using a paddle and helping with the droghing. Accordingly he travelled up with the doctor to Kaieteur, who, when he had looked at the falls and taken a spool of photographs, descended (incidentally cracking a rib en route) and left Sacramento alone at the top. On looking about for the road he had been promised he found it to be nonexistent; the plateau ended in impenetrable bush; the only craft at the landing was Winter's boat – far too heavy to be launched, still less propelled upstream, single-handed. So Sacramento found himself without provisions or hope of escape until the next tourist should arrive, perhaps in six months' time.

Fortunately for him, Winter was on his way back to the diamond working, and ten days later met Sacramento, by then within a fine distance of death from starvation and poisoning from the roots and berries he had been attempting to eat. Winter fed him by increasing degrees until he was restored to a fair state of health and then sent him back to Amatuk in his boat, but Sacramento took the kindness with little gratitude. With returning strength, his wanderlust came back to him and he could not be persuaded that the road into Brazil was quite impossible to a man without guides and provisions, that the Indians were scattered, elusive and quite unwilling, even when they were able, to give food to strange foreigners. Sacramento went back under compulsion, alive but full of resentment.

It was interesting to notice the reactions to Kaieteur of the different members of the party. Gerry and the two Indian boys had seen it before and did not bother to look again. Sobers had been there seven times but always went down to see it, with genuine awe and appreciation of its beauty. The Patamona family had never been there before and did not take the smallest interest in it; instead they lit the fire under their hammocks and lay alternately dozing and munching *farine* without putting themselves quarter of a mile out of the way to see it. One book says that the Indians think it haunted by *Kenaima* and, when obliged to approach, put pepper in their eyes to blind themselves, but I heard no confirmation of this and I think the Patamonas' reluctance to visit it came from mere stupidity and lack of imagination.

Next morning, as soon as it was light, Sobers and I went down to the fall, this time not to the ledge from which I had seen it the night before, but down another line to the water edge, where we were able to walk on dry rocks to the very brink of the fall. But at that time the whole basin and gorge were full of mist that blotted out everything except the rush of brown water at our feet.

As before, the bad family lay long in their hammocks and pottered about with wood embers and fish preparing a lengthy breakfast. There was a long, very steep, rocky descent to Tokeit landing. On the way we passed a snake, coiled up asleep in the trail, bathed at the bottom and launched the boat while we waited for the Indians to arrive. The boat proved to be of the same build as the one we had used the day before, but about half its size, and quite incapable of carrying the whole of the party. Accordingly I decided to leave the bad family behind. They accepted their desertion with the same brutish apathy they had shown to all our proceedings. They had rations for two days which we were able to supplement very slightly from the remaining stores. It would be at least five days, probably longer, before Gerry returned from Kangaruma to relieve them. Meanwhile they were better off than Alfredo Sacramento because they had a bow and arrows with them; there was fish in the river and no doubt game in the bush, and, anyway, periodic fasts are common enough experiences in their own villages. Nevertheless I felt guilty, though less guilty than I had done in the case of Eusebio. Some of the party *had* to be left behind and they and their dog were the most easily spared. They squatted at the water's edge and watched us till we were out of sight.

Lightened as we were, the boat was dangerously low in the water and our progress correspondingly slow. It was windless in the gorge and now we began to feel the weight of the descent we had made. Days and nights grew hotter the nearer we approached the coast. After Kangaruma there was no need for a blanket at night, and the briskness we had felt in the hills gave way to lassitude.

The gorge, which from Kaieteur had the appearance of a single cleft, was revealed on closer acquaintance as a series of wooded hills. The river wound in and out between them until at noon we reached Waratuk. At high flood these rapids could be shot, but at this season it had the effect of a dam of boulders spanning the river with, between each, a sharp cataract, bubbling over rocks in a series of little falls and whirlpools. The broadest channel was on the left bank. We drew the boat in, unloaded it and carried the stores to a sand beach that lay in still water quarter of a mile downstream. Here the Indians and I waited while Gerry and Sobers handled the boat over the rapids. They tied a rope to the stern, hitched it round a boulder, and Sobers took the end, slowly paying it out under Gerry's orders. Gerry stood at the bows, and, sometimes jumping from stone to stone, sometimes wading thigh-deep in the surf, steered them between the rocks. If he had lost his footing and loosed his hold on the boat for a moment, it would have been swept sideways and stove in. The whole operation took about twenty minutes and was done with astonishing dexterity and absence of fuss. In a few days' time Gerry would have the far more difficult task of taking the boat up, without Sobers' help. I wondered how he would manage it; so, I think, did Gerry, looking contemptuously at the frail little Indians who would be his companions.

We cooked lunch on the sandbank, rested for an hour and then reloaded the boat and set out again. In about three hours we reached Amatuk, where the boat was no further use to us and had to be beached. It was here that trouble might be expected with Mr Diabolo. He lived on the right bank some way below the falls, and we were just walking down to shout across to him when we heard ourselves hailed from behind and saw some blacks fishing among the rocks. They appeared to be friends of Sobers. In a few minutes one of them appeared in a boat and rowed over to us. He was a youth of unmistakably criminal appearance, but he greeted Sobers and Gerry with great warmth, and bowed politely to me. We got into the boat with our baggage, picked up the fishermen and presently made for a house on the further bank. This, I gathered, was Mr Diabolo's boat, and that was Mr Diabolo's house. Mr Diabolo was away, so both these had been appropriated by our friends who were 'pork knockers' washing the gravel of a worked-out diamond claim that had once belonged to Winter. They were as open-handed to us as they had been to themselves, and readily let us have the use of the boat for our journey to Kangaruma on the next day. The presence of the friendly 'pork knockers' was doubly fortunate, for it solved the problem which had worried my conscience far more than the discomfort of the bad Patamona family: that was how, without them, Winter's stores were to be carried in reasonable time up Amatuk and Waratuk. For a dollar a head the blacks agreed to take on the job.

They also urged us to sleep in Mr Diabolo's house, but there was another slightly lower down, belonging to Mrs McTurk, where I thought I should be more comfortable. It was built on a small island in the middle of the river; at flood time this was submerged and the house stood up in midstream on its piles just clear of the water. There was an armchair there, the first I had seen for many weeks, and a shelf of tattered novels. An aged Negro lived there as caretaker and exacted a toll of one dollar for its use. The vampires in that house were thicker than I had found them anywhere, and kept me awake by fluttering round my mosquito net and hanging to it, trying to nose a way in.

But the armchair and the row of old novels, and the caretaker with his white woolly head, his respectful English and his expectation of a tip, were all symbols of the return to civilization; another phase of the journey – the last but one – was over.

NINE

Compared with the country above Kaieteur, the lower Potaro was
populous and civilized. With every splash of the paddles we drew
nearer to Georgetown, not only in mileage but in the air and temper
of our surroundings; we passed other boats manned by Negroes in
felt hats, vests and short trousers; we were among people who spoke
English and knew the value of money; the buildings were graced
with corrugated iron, wire fencing, asbestos and sawn planks. But it
was a broken and fugitive civilization. Not here those firm, confident
tentacles of modernity that extend to greet the traveller; no tractors
making their own roads as they advance; no progressive young
managers projecting more advanced stations of commerce, opening
up new districts, pushing forward new settlements and new markets;
no uniformed law asserting itself in chaos.

Instead we had overtaken civilization in its retreat; the ground
was worked out, the beaches sifted of their treasure, the trees bled
to death for ballata, the stores derelict and once busy stations in
process of evacuation. It was as though modernity had put out
sensitive snail-horns and, being hurt, had withdrawn them. The
wounds in the bush – surface scratches negligible to its vast bulk and
power – were healing over and the place returning to solitude and
desolation frivolously disturbed.

There had once been a police station below Amatuk and a handful
of shops trading rum and rations for gold dust, diamonds and
ballata. These and the clusters of shacks round them had all been
abandoned in the retrocession; the rain and the ants and the
omnivorous bush were pulling them to pieces and overwhelming
them. They were very ignoble ruins; not the majestic façades of the

burned-out houses of Southern Ireland or the overgrown capitals and pediments that remain when a real civilization comes to its end; bare frames of rotten timber and misshapen tin or, most desolate of all, rusted and half-buried heaps of useless machinery. For it was a destructive and predatory civilization that we were meeting, and it was disappearing like the trenches and shell-craters of a battlefield.

At Kangaruma I came once more into contact with regular communications, though not, let it be said, communications highly organized or very direct. Here the river made a wide detour over impassable waterfalls. A broad trail had been cut through to Potaro landing and the intervening creeks roughly bridged, forming the straight five-mile base of a triangle. A lorry covered this journey when freight warranted and the state of its mechanism permitted it. As often as not the vehicle was out of order and passengers were obliged to walk; this had been the case when Sobers was last there and he expressed little confidence in its restoration. From Potaro landing a launch with an outboard engine plied, when required, to Tumatumari, where there was a village and another waterfall. From Tumatumari there was another motor launch owned by an East Indian which journeyed irregularly to Rockstone on the Essequibo where there had once been a village and a railway service to Wismar. Trains no longer ran, but the line remained and it was possible to cross either by foot or on a truck pushed by hand or, if one was fortunate, drawn by a motor tractor. Wismar was a place of some importance on the Demerara, where an American company were working for bauxite, and from there bi-weekly steamers sailed to Georgetown. It will be clear that the journey involved a number of somewhat uncertain connections. It was, however, a definite line of communication and in that differed from anything I had encountered since leaving the Berbice.

There was also an alternative route down the government's new road to Bartika, which met the Potaro at a point between Potaro landing and Tumatumari. Something has been said of this enterprise already and comment is apposite here after what I have written above about the abandonment of the district, for there certainly was a large scheme making for its development. The next ten years or so will show which will be victor, the bush or the road. It is being done at what is, for the Colony, great expense and on a considerable scale, and is, in its way, a courageous attempt. If it is unsuccessful, the defeat will mean the abandonment at any rate for a generation, probably for ever, of the 'opening up' of the interior; the Colony will resign itself to the limits of a single strip of seaboard and leave the huge territory at its back in the primeval integrity it has always maintained.

The arguments against its success may be stated as follows: that it was too late in coming; twenty years earlier when the Potaro was busy with 'pork knockers', ballata bleeders and quite a few gold seekers working on a large scale, it might have been of immense value – by now the district was too far decayed and its resources exhausted; that it was unreliable from an engineering point of view being built on sand over a substructure of roots – it would subside and collapse, the sand would wash away and the government would be faced with the alternative of abandoning wheeled traffic or spending a great sum annually in its upkeep; that since it was a ridge road – running partly along natural hills and partly on an artificial viaduct – there was little prospect of settlers cultivating its borders, for the difficulties of transporting produce to the road level would counterbalance the advantage of rapid transit; that even as it was the journey to Georgetown took as long that way as by Rockstone, for it was a two-day land journey, and boats ran from Bartika just as infrequently as from Wismar; moreover, the journey was one of excruciating discomfort, with every possibility of a breakdown on the way and an indefinite delay in the bush. At the time Sobers, who found a mournful pleasure in multiplying the probable difficulties of our journey, had come up, there had been a two weeks' cessation of the lorry service.

Whatever the ultimate advantages of the new road, I decided in the immediate circumstances to follow the river route. At Kangaruma the prospect was more hopeful than Sobers had led me to expect, for the lorry to Potaro landing was in order and due to start on the next day and there seemed a very fair chance of all the connections fitting and my getting to Georgetown on the fourth day.

There was a shop at Kangaruma where I was able to purchase tinned butter (at seven and sixpence a pound), corned beef, potatoes, fairly fresh bread, tobacco, beer and other luxuries. There was a clean room kept for visitors, a good bathing creek and, most remarkable of all a pile of newspapers, the weekly edition of an illustrated daily dating to within a month of my arrival. I had not seen an English paper later than the one I read on board ship on the morning of my departure from London. Inevitably, I had come to expect every kind of public and private cataclysm, the fall of governments, outbreak of wars and revolutions, the assassination of the royal family, the marriage, parenthood, divorce and death of all my friends. Actually, of course, it was a very short time and nothing of particular note had occurred. But, even so, it was the newspapers more than anything else that brought it home to me that my journey was coming to an end.

It did not end without some remaining asperities. Now that one was back among organized communications, all the civilized man's impatience at delay returned and each stage of the journey was attended by several hours' irritation during which the various Negroes responsible came nearly to blows in apparently pointless altercations. The lorry, however, was ready next morning and, after immense preliminary agitation of the starting handle, was got to work and arrived at its destination late but intact.

I left Gerry and the Indians sorting out Winter's stores. Sobers, as arranged, came on with me. From Amatuk onwards our relations became remote; he said 'Chief' more often when talking to me and took off his cap whenever he came into a room where I was sitting. There had been an inevitable transition; we were no longer travelling companions but servant and master.

There was a long wait at Potaro landing while the captain of the boat and the driver of the lorry attempted to remove part of the engine which had to be taken down-river for repairs. They quarrelled with one another, shouted at the tops of their voices and knocked the car about in a way which must have shortened its already precariously protracted existence by a considerable time. Finally when they had battered and hammered and wrenched and roared themselves hoarse they gave up the attempt as hopeless and we chugged down towards Tumatumari. After a mile or two we came to Garroway stream, the present terminus of the government road. There was a large labour camp there and the beginnings of a bridge which, if the venture continues, will carry the road up to Kaieteur. We took on mail and a couple more passengers and reached Tumatumari at half-past one.

This had once been a considerable town with an hotel, police station and resident commissioner; now it was a ramshackle Negro village of wooden huts sprawling along one street that led past the falls between the two landings. The only man of any authority was an aged and amiable black who combined the offices of postmaster, schoolteacher and preacher. There was a little rest house, maintained for the use of visiting officials, to which he gave me the keys. He also lent me a romance of colonial life written by a black schoolmaster and printed in Trinidad – a curiously ingenuous tale of the finally reconciled conflict of love and duty.

There were a dozen or so stores in the village licensed to buy gold and sell rum, and a chattering black population who lived on supplying recreation to 'pork knockers'. At first there was no news of the Rockstone boat whose timetable, apparently, depended on the caprice of the bosun. 'Him starts when him likes,' they said. 'De captain very old and him can't see much.'

But it arrived that afternoon with a handful of passengers. One of them had brought a live pig. He was a speculator in pork and it was his practice to borrow a pig from the station clerk at Rockstone, bring it to Tumatumari and lead it about the village, hawking for orders. The price was fixed beforehand. If he got enough orders for meat to cover his fare and show a small profit, he killed the pig, divided it up and returned to pay its owner. If there was no adequate market, he led the animal back disconsolately to Rockstone and was the loser by the expense of his journey. On this occasion the demand was brisk, and the beast's death squeals disturbed the evening.

I went down to the landing, interviewed the all powerful bosun and extorted a promise from him to sail at seven the next morning. It was essential to make an early start if we were to catch the Wismar boat, which left early the following morning. A few hours' delay might mean the loss of four days in a town where I was reluctant to spend much time.

Next morning at seven, however, there was no sign of activity at the landing, and the stores we were taking down still lay in a heap on shore. I recruited Sobers and some other passengers and got the boat loaded, but the bosun still maintained that he was unable to start; the mailbag had not arrived. I went up to the post office and found it open and the postmaster still accepting letters, which arrived in a dilatory fashion every quarter of an hour. Everyone who bought a stamp felt herself – they were mostly women – entitled to a several minutes' gossip. A large printed order announced that on the mornings when the mail left, the office was closed at 6.30 a.m. I pointed this out and demanded that the bag be sent down to the boat. The postmaster explained that he had to sort all the letters out first, complete his own correspondence and seal up the bag. Meanwhile more Negresses came slopping up, flat-footed, to buy postal orders and chat about their families. It was eleven before we started.

It took us ten hours to Rockstone without a stop. I sat under an awning amidships. There was one other first-class passenger, a large black lady of some importance, for she wore shoes and gold earrings and travelled with a bag of peppermints and a thermos flask of cold water. The men at the back lit a fire on a piece of iron and cooked luncheon on the way.

After we reached the Essequibo the scenery became painfully monotonous – a vast breadth of water bordered by forest and broken occasionally by islands of bush. After dark my companion slept, sprawling over most of the seat.

Rockstone was another deserted town. The large wooden house built as an hotel was falling to pieces; beside it stood the barrack-like quarters that had been used by the railway employees. The only inhabitant now was the East Indian railway clerk who lived in the derelict station. I explained to him the urgency of my catching the Demerara boat. He was full of sympathy, remarking that Rockstone and Wismar were full of mosquitoes and no place in which to spend unnecessary nights. He was himself shaking with fever. It was impossible, however, to get across that night, he said, as the tractor was out of order.

I interviewed the bosun of the boat, who seemed the only active man about, and the driver of the tractor; they were both despondent until I offered five dollars between them if I caught the ship next morning. That secured their attention and for some hours grinding noises, sudden reports and showers of sparks came from the stationary tractor. Meanwhile the other passengers, about twelve in all, had retired to sleep, some of them hanging hammocks from convenient posts, some making little nests among the heaps of goods which littered the yard, others sprawling, without compromise, across the platform. I put up my hammock in the booking office and went to sleep with little expectation of getting to Wismar until next day.

Just before midnight, however, the clerk began running up and down the platform shaking the sleepers and blowing his whistle. The tractor was working.

We all climbed with our luggage into an open trolley and with a grating of gears and overwhelming issue of exhaust gas, the tractor started.

It was a slow journey; the oil lamp that hung in front of us illumined little except the two rails. The bush had originally been cut back some distance on either side to protect the line from falling timber, but a luxurious second growth now grew round and over us. Two or three times we were obliged to stop and remove fallen branches and shovel away a small landslide. After two hours it came on to rain heavily and passengers drew a tarpaulin sheet over us, completely excluding air and view. Personally I would have preferred a wetting. I have occasionally heard it debated whether Negroes have an unpleasant smell. These certainly had. I have also heard it said that white men are as disagreeable to them as they are to us; I can only say that my fellow passengers on this journey were not fastidious and showed no desire to avoid proximity with me. I could have wished they had.

But it came to an end at last, a little before dawn. The Demerara boat was at the quayside and we went on board at once and dozed in a swarm of mosquitoes.

Next day we sailed downstream with a perceptible sea breeze in our faces, past sugar plantations, bovianders' huts, East India villages – characteristic riverside scenery. Early that afternoon I was back in Georgetown.

The journey was over and here the book might well come to an end. There is no occasion for a purple passage. I have written throughout a direct and, I hope, accurate day-to-day chronicle of a journey over strange ground and in circumstances that were – to me – unusual. It makes no claim to being a spiritual odyssey. Whatever interior changes there were – and all experience makes some change – are the writer's own property and not a marketable commodity. I had been ninety-two days away from letters and the normal amenities of life; it had been an arduous and at times arid experience. I had taken enough strenuous exercise and suffered enough mild privation to justify myself in spending the rest of the year in indolence and self-indulgence. I had one grave breach of faith – poor Eusebio – on my conscience. I had contributed to the generally distasteful impressions of the new prior of Boa Vista. I had caused unavoidable pain to several horses. I had added to my treasury of eccentrics the fantastic figure of Mr Christie. I had seen several different sorts of life being led – rancher, missionary, Indian, diamond hunter – which I could never have imagined. I had added another small piece to the pages of the atlas that were real to me. For me it had been abundantly worth while, and it seems to me conceivable that an account of it may interest some people. I might make this the end of the book and abandon for good the nursery where I have been working, but I think it would be in keeping with its desultory nature to complete it, as it has been written, with some final, unambitious paragraphs about the remaining days.

There was some time to wait in Georgetown before there was a ship home. Even then I had to break my voyage at Trinidad. In Georgetown I met an agreeable character called 'Professor' Piles who lived by selling stuffed alligators. He had a peculiar fascination over them and over snakes, and loved both species dearly. He used to go out to the creeks and call them; it went greatly against his sentiments to kill them, but he had to live. Once he had been put in prison at Mazaruni and had secured release by the simple expedient of summoning every snake in the neighbourhood. Every morning when the warders came to his cell they found it full of assembled reptiles. They would accompany him at recreation and at work to the great detriment of good order and discipline, so that eventually the Governor was obliged to order his release. I bought a crate full of baby alligators from him to take back as presents to the children of my friends. They have not been a great success. One child said, foolishly, I thought, 'Is it a rabbit?' and another – a girl – called it 'Evelyn' and proceeded to tear it to pieces; a third said, 'Is it real?' and on being told that it was asked, 'Is it dead?' His interest was then exhausted and he returned to his bricks.

I renewed the acquaintances I had made at Christmas and paid formal calls of farewell, feeling a little patronizing towards the town dwellers who let themselves be shut in between forest and sea and never adventured into the country behind them.

'Have you been up to Kaieteur?'

'Not exactly, but I passed it coming down, on my way back.'

There was the inevitable disappointment of getting my films back from the developers. I had taken two dozen rolls and packed them with every precaution Father Mather or I could devise, but many of them had got spoiled during the journey. A large number, too, were failures as pictures. Without exception all the photographs taken in the bush and in the cattle trail were worthless, pitch-dark with glaring blots of light. Even those in which the exposure had been successful were disappointing, for compositions which had seemed full of interest when I took them now appeared drab and insignificant. All the landscapes, except those of river scenery, were despoiled of their beauty, the hills flattened out, the trees barely distinguishable, the valleys without form. The Indians had been, as I have described, elusive subjects, but I had taken numerous snapshots of them unawares by the device which I may commend to the more careful manipulations of others facing the same problem; you stand or sit facing at right angles to your subject and holding the camera sideways, turned towards them, looking ahead but all the time glancing down and sighting the lens by means of the finder. The Indians rarely suspected that they were being taken, nor alas, would these suspicions have been aroused in most cases if they had seen the results, which, though amusing souvenirs, were few of them recognizable as portraits and fewer still reproducible as the illustrations for which they were primarily intended.

Out of 192 exposures, barely fifty were of any real interest.

From Georgetown to Trinidad in a smart Canadian ship, full of seasick boy scouts on their way to a Jamboree, and convivial golfers going to a tournament in Barbados.

It was Holy Week, so I went out to stay in a little Benedictine monastery in the hills behind Port of Spain. They maintain a guest house where many people go for the cool air. I sat at table with a lady anthropologist with whom I involved myself in acrimonious arguments about Indian character. She would not have it that they were cowards, and she knew much more of them than I did; but I still think I was right.

I feel that this book has too much ecclesiastical flavour already; otherwise I could well devote a chapter to the Easter festivals at Mount St Benedict. On Good Friday pilgrims of all races and creeds assembled to kiss the Cross from all parts of the island – Hindus, Protestants, Chinese – and for Easter morning the church and courtyard of the monastery were packed with a dense crowd. They began arriving at about ten on Saturday evening, and all through the night we could hear the chatter and the padding of bare feet as they climbed past the guest house. The first Mass was said before dawn, and after it the great crowd formed a procession, each carrying a candle in a coloured paper shade. As the only white man present I found a torch thrust into my hands to carry in front of the Host. The line of coloured lights wound down the steeply graded hill road and climbed back again to the church, and just as we reached the summit again day began to break over the hills and there was a feeling of New Year.

From Trinidad I took a comfortable Dutch ship to Southampton. There was some slight discussion at the Customs as to whether stuffed alligators were dutiable as furniture, but in the end these were allowed in as scientific specimens. After a change of luggage in London I went straight to Bath and spent a week there alone in an hotel. Spring was breaking in the gardens, tender and pure and very different from the gross vegetation of the tropics. I had seen no building that was stable or ancient for nearly six months. Bath, with its propriety and uncompromised grandeur, seemed to offer everything that was most valuable in English life; and there, pottering composedly among the squares and crescents, I came finally to the end of my journey.

MORE ABOUT PENGUINS, PELICANS, PEREGRINES AND PUFFINS

For further information about books available from Penguins please write to Dept EP, Penguin Books Ltd, Harmondsworth, Middlesex UB7 0DA.

In the U.S.A.: For a complete list of books available from Penguins in the United States write to Dept DG, Penguin Books, 299 Murray Hill Parkway, East Rutherford, New Jersey 07073.

In Canada: For a complete list of books available from Penguins in Canada write to Penguin Books Canada Ltd, 2801 John Street, Markham, Ontario L3R 1B4.

In Australia: For a complete list of books available from Penguins in Australia write to the Marketing Department, Penguin Books Australia Ltd, P.O. Box 257, Ringwood, Victoria 3134.

In New Zealand: For a complete list of books available from Penguins in New Zealand write to the Marketing Department, Penguin Books (N.Z.) Ltd, Private Bag, Takapuna, Auckland 9.

In India: For a complete list of books available from Penguins in India write to Penguin Overseas Ltd, 706 Eros Apartments, 56 Nehru Place, New Delhi 110019.

LABELS

Evelyn Waugh chose the name *Labels* for his first travel book because, he said, the places he visited were already 'fully labelled' in people's minds.

But even the most seasoned traveller could not fail to be inspired by Waugh's quintessentially English attitude and by his eloquent and frequently outrageous wit. From Europe to the Middle East to North Africa, from Egytian porters and Italian priests to Maltese sailors and Moroccan merchants – as he cruises around the Mediterranean his pen cuts through the local colour to give a highly entertaining portrait of the Englishman abroad.

Written in 1929, *Labels* is a splendid example of the genius that was to make its author the greatest writer of his generation.

'He will be admired as long as there are people who can read' – *Daily Telegraph*

REMOTE PEOPLE

In 1930 Evelyn Waugh went out to Abyssinia as special correspondent for *The Times* to cover the coronation of the Emperor Ras Tafari – Haile Selassie I, King of the Kings of Ethiopia.

This is Waugh's fascinating account, not just of Ethiopia and the coronation, but of his subsequent travels in Aden, Kenya, Zanzibar, the Belgian Congo and South Africa. The countryside, cities, towns and villages are vividly described and just as vividly populated: natives rub shoulders on Waugh's pages with eccentric expatriates, settlers with Arab traders and dignitaries with Armenian monks.

Brilliant, amusing and truthful, Evelyn Waugh combines clear-edged observation and honesty in this wonderful travelogue, interspersing his tales with three 'nightmares' which describe the frustrations of travel and the disappointment of returning home.

and
Waugh in Abyssinia

Evelyn Waugh in Penguins

DECLINE AND FALL
VILE BODIES
BLACK MISCHIEF
A HANDFUL OF DUST
PUT OUT MORE FLAGS
SCOOP
THE LOVED ONE
THE ORDEAL OF GILBERT PINFOLD
AND OTHER STORIES
MEN AT ARMS
OFFICERS AND GENTLEMEN
UNCONDITIONAL SURRENDER
WHEN THE GOING WAS GOOD
WORK SUSPENDED WITH CHARLES RYDER'S
SCHOOLDAYS AND OTHER STORIES

and

THE DIARIES OF EVELYN WAUGH

EDITED BY MICHAEL DAVIE

'An extraordinary, perhaps unique document, self-revealing, indeed often self-lacerating ... perceptive and stylish ... Bibulous and pious, gossip-gathering and gossip-provoking, pugnacious and scholarly, callous and touchy, it is the work of a haunted man' Alan Brien in the *Sunday Times*

THE LETTERS OF EVELYN WAUGH

EDITED BY MARK AMORY

'A joy to read riveting, subtle, outrageously funny, honest and touching the effect is that of a work of great art, a self-portrait fit to hold its own beside anything by Rembrandt or Van Gogh' *Literary Review*

'Some 650 pages of elegant gossip, ferocious malice, high seriousness, social observation and sheer lunacy (both real and inspired)' *Sunday Telegraph*

A CHOICE OF PENGUINS

☐ *Small World* **David Lodge**   £2.50

A jet-propelled academic romance, sequel to *Changing Places*. 'A new comic débâcle on every page' – *The Times*. 'Here is everything one expects from Lodge but three times as entertaining as anything he has written before' – *Sunday Telegraph*

☐ *The Neverending Story* **Michael Ende**   £3.50

The international bestseller, now a major film: 'A tale of magical adventure, pursuit and delay, danger, suspense, triumph' – *The Times Literary Supplement*

☐ *The Sword of Honour Trilogy* **Evelyn Waugh**   £3.95

Containing *Men at Arms, Officers and Gentlemen* and *Unconditional Surrender*, the trilogy described by Cyril Connolly as 'unquestionably the finest novels to have come out of the war'.

☐ *The Honorary Consul* **Graham Greene**   £1.95

In a provincial Argentinian town, a group of revolutionaries kidnap the wrong man . . . 'The tension never relaxes and one reads hungrily from page to page, dreading the moment it will all end' – Auberon Waugh in the *Evening Standard*

☐ *The First Rumpole Omnibus* **John Mortimer**   £4.95

Containing *Rumpole of the Bailey, The Trials of Rumpole* and *Rumpole's Return*. 'A fruity, foxy masterpiece, defender of our wilting faith in mankind' – *Sunday Times*

☐ *Scandal* **A. N. Wilson**   £2.25

Sexual peccadillos, treason and blackmail are all ingredients on the boil in A. N. Wilson's new, *cordon noir* comedy. 'Drily witty, deliciously nasty' – *Sunday Telegraph*

A CHOICE OF PENGUINS

☐ **Stanley and the Women** Kingsley Amis   £2.50

'Very good, very powerful . . . beautifully written . . . This is Amis *père* at his best' – Anthony Burgess in the *Observer*. 'Everybody should read it' – *Daily Mail*

☐ **The Mysterious Mr Ripley** Patricia Highsmith   £4.95

Containing *The Talented Mr Ripley, Ripley Underground* and *Ripley's Game*. 'Patricia Highsmith is the poet of apprehension' – Graham Greene. 'The Ripley books are marvellously, insanely readable' – *The Times*

☐ **Earthly Powers** Anthony Burgess   £4.95

'Crowded, crammed, bursting with manic erudition, garlicky puns, omnilingual jokes . . . (a novel) which meshes the real and personalized history of the twentieth century' – Martin Amis

☐ **Life & Times of Michael K** J. M. Coetzee   £2.95

The Booker Prize-winning novel: 'It is hard to convey . . . just what Coetzee's special quality is. His writing gives off whiffs of Conrad, of Nabokov, of Golding, of the Paul Theroux of *The Mosquito Coast*. But he is none of these, he is a harsh, compelling new voice' – Victoria Glendinning

☐ **The Stories of William Trevor**   £5.95

'Trevor packs into each separate five or six thousand words more richness, more laughter, more ache, more multifarious human-ness than many good writers manage to get into a whole novel' – *Punch*

☐ **The Book of Laughter and Forgetting**
Milan Kundera   £3.95

'A whirling dance of a book . . . a masterpiece full of angels, terror, ostriches and love . . . No question about it. The most important novel published in Britain this year' – Salman Rushdie

A CHOICE OF PENGUINS

☐ *The Philosopher's Pupil* **Iris Murdoch**   £2.95

'We are back, of course, with great delight, in the land of Iris Murdoch, which is like no other but Prospero's . . .' – *Sunday Telegraph*. And, as expected, her latest masterpiece is 'marvellous . . . compulsive reading, hugely funny' – *Spectator*

☐ *A Good Man in Africa* **William Boyd**   £2.50

Boyd's brilliant, award-winning frolic featuring Morgan Leafy, overweight, oversexed representative of Her Britannic Majesty in tropical Kinjanja. 'Wickedly funny' – *The Times*

These books should be available at all good bookshops or newsagents, but if you live in the UK or the Republic of Ireland and have difficulty in getting to a bookshop, they can be ordered by post. Please indicate the titles required and fill in the form below.

NAME _____ BLOCK CAPITALS

ADDRESS _____

_____

_____

Enclose a cheque or postal order payable to The Penguin Bookshop to cover the total price of books ordered, plus 50p for postage. Readers in the Republic of Ireland should send £IR equivalent to the sterling prices, plus 67p for postage. Send to: The Penguin Bookshop, 54/56 Bridlesmith Gate, Nottingham, NG1 2GP.

You can also order by phoning (0602) 599295, and quoting your Barclaycard or Access number.

Every effort is made to ensure the accuracy of the price and availability of books at the time of going to press, but it is sometimes necessary to increase prices and in these circumstances retail prices may be shown on the covers of books which may differ from the prices shown in this list or elsewhere. This list is not an offer to supply any book.

This order service is only available to residents in the UK and the Republic of Ireland.

● ● ●